GIS Guidebook:

DESIGNING AND BUILDING TASKS

for ArcGIS Pro

By David W. Allen, GISP

GIS Guidebooks Press

Published by GIS Guidebooks Press

Corsicana, TX

ISBN-13: 978-0-578-47838-8

About the Author

David Allen has been working with GIS since 1983, developed the GIS system for the City of Euless and has worked there over 30 years, taught evening classes in the GIS program at Tarrant County College for over 19 years, and has published several other bestselling books on GIS. He knows this stuff inside and out … and he has a great knack at being able to explain complex topics in a simple way. He has been working with ArcGIS Pro since the first Beta, has traveled to Redlands many times to work with the developers and test these new tools, and is continually working on new methods and ideas of how this stuff can best be put to best use.

Gis Guidebook: Designing and Building Tasks in ArcGIS Pro

Table of Contents

Author's Introduction

You will need to download the datasets for this book in order to complete all the exercises. Check the book's page at **http://www.GisGuidebooks.com/Tasks** for more information and a link to download the files.

It's impossible to only use workflows that are common to all GIS users as examples and exercises in this book, so my advice when working through this book is to focus on how processes are handled and how the settings are used with regard to the task . If you don't understand a workflow or why it's done a certain way (or if you normally do it a different way) at least pay attention to how that workflow is being integrated into a task with the takeaway being how to use and understand the steps and techniques being shown. It is also helpful to immediately apply this knowledge in your own working environment so that you can personalize it to your daily activities. You should also check the GISGuidebooks.com website periodically for blog posts on helpful topics, including new ways to use tasks.

The examples and exercises that are presented here are totally fictional and while they may seem to follow realistic practices, they shouldn't be used as a guide for designing your own workflows. Some of the tasks may follow a workflow or use processes that aren't the most efficient or intuitive, but each is designed to highlight particular components and techniques that are used in the task structure. If you examine one of theworkflows and have a better way to do it, go ahead and work through the process the way the book describes to learn the specific techniques highlighted. Afterwards you can design your own workflow and build a new task to accomplish it using your own methods. This would be good practice for you.

It is expected that you already know how to use ArcGIS Pro before starting this book. No instruction will be given on how to open project documents, how to access menu tools, how to search and run Geoprocessing tools, etc … If you are not comfortable working in ArcGIS Pro then I would suggest starting with a book on that topic. It's also helpful to know the ArcGIS Pro terminology. Here's a few that are used in this book:

Pane—the pop-up box or window that opens with a tool or menu selection.

Ribbon menu—the large, tabbed menu across the top of the screen.

Context menu—the menu that opens when you right-click on an item such as a layer, folder or tool.

Docking—the action of securing a menu or tool with another tool in the same pane.

Geoprocessing Pane—opens from the Analysis > Tools icon on the Ribbon menu.

Dialog box—the line in a tool's window where you type in a value.

Throughout the book you will also see "Rafael's Question" which is a question students "Rafael's Dilemma" classroom except in this situation I have to both ask and answer them. You will also find sections where you will take techniques that were just described and apply them to a new task with minimalinstruction. Helpful tips are given that you can reference as you solve the dilemma.

Not everyone is a programmer (and that's not a bad thing) and this book won't turn you into a programmer. But you will probably learn to think more like a programmer – in a more step-by-step, linear fashion. In the end, however, I think you will be very surprised at how much customizing and automating you can do without being a programmer or even writing a single line of code.

DWA

Chapter 1 - The Mechanics of Tasks

Introduction to workflow and process automation – Tasks vs. Models

There are many jobs and projects that you do in GIS that can get repetitive or require precise steps in a certain order, and each time you face one of these jobs you think "Is there a way to make this easier"? The answer is yes, and the best part is that you don't have to be a programmer to do it. Within ArcGIS Pro are two components for storing workflows and building a user interface so that anyone can easily repeat the workflow. They are tasks, new for ArcGIS Pro, and models, using ModelBuilder which has been around for some time. But what are the differences between tasks and models?

Think of tasks as being an interactive management tool, and models as being an automated management tool. A task contains a list of steps you would do in a particular workflow or process and it feeds them back to you when run, stopping when necessary to get user interaction such as selecting a feature or providing a value. On the other hand models can prompt for user input before they start, but once you run them they do not allow for any additional user interaction and each step must be completed in order.

Another big difference is that tasks can only do things that a user at the keyboard could do. A task can use any Ribbon menu tool, access parameters for layers or the project environment, run a geoprocessing tool, and control this through a list of steps that the user can manage. And while a model can't do all of the things a task can relating to the project interface, it can do a wide variety of things that a task can't. For instance, a model can make a decision based on an attribute value and steer the workflow a different way; or it can iterate through features (or even feature classes) and perform processes on a large number of features without interaction; or many other programming-like functions that make it very flexible. The limitation is that models can only do these things using geoprocessing tools – none of the menu commands are available to a model.

But then there's the best of both worlds ... a task can call a model as one of its steps. That means that if, for instance, your task gets to a point in its workflow where it needs to act upon all the feature classes in a workspace, you can write a model to do that and call it from the task. This is a very simplistic and conceptual description of these items, and as you progress through this book you will gain a better and more thorough understanding of when to use a task, when to use a model, and when to combine them.

What makes a good task?

There are several reasons why you might want to make one of your workflows or processes into a task. You may want to document the best practices for the workflow and make certain that all users are doing the processes correctly. When users run the task, they will be guided step-by-step through the workflow and not have the opportunity to vary any of the processes. For example, the owner notification process for changing the zoning on a parcel of land has a very strict process that must be followed. Otherwise the resulting zoning change may be considered illegal or invalid. By using a task you can ensure that all processes are completed according to the legal specifications.

Tasks may also be used to document a process that isn't done very frequently. For instance, the monthly summary of road traffic counts may be very complex and remembering all the steps is both problematic and critical. Each time the task is used you can be assured that no steps were omitted. This also contributes to your data integrity plan. Any user in your organization can run the report and you can be certain that all of the parameters for all of the processes are set correctly, and that all of the data is ultimately stored in the correct format and location. Imagine trying to do a month-to-month comparison of the summary results if the steps were not uniform.

There are several characteristics of a good task. It should be a workflow of definable steps, it should be something that is repeated often, and something that the user would normally go through step by step at the keyboard. If a workflow requires too much decision making by the user or changes frequently, then it may not make a good candidate for a task. Likewise, if a workflow is very long or requires complex geoprocessing it may need to be split into several tasks or even include a model for advanced functions.

Designing tasks

The process of designing and building a task starts with knowing the background of what this task needs to accomplish. You will need to know the actions you take in great detail, even to the point of knowing how the ArcGIS Pro project file is set up. Imagine yourself at the keyboard performing this workflow unguided. You will set certain configurations within the project file itself, and set up the layers for use. This might include which toolbars to work from; which layers are in the Contents pane and what data they represent; the selectability, visibility, edit state, and snapping for all layers; and which locations to use for data storage. It's also important to know if or when any of these parameters change during the course of the workflow. If someone else were to repeat your workflow, you would want them to have the same parameters set in their project file that you normally use.

Next you need to understand the steps you follow in the workflow. What are you doing and why – and in what order? Each button click and keyboard stroke will be duplicated in the task, and each menu tool or geoprocessing tool that you use will also be included. You will need to go through the workflow slowly and consciously think about everything you do, and document it. If you forget a step and don't put it in the task, then others won't repeat your workflow as you expected. This is a very important step in the design process because it will not only provide the blueprint for the task but also supply the description of each step that may be used in the documentation.

And the final concern in designing a task is to know who will be using it. Will this be used by the general public, an uninformed user who has limited knowledge of the workflow, or by an expert in the field who understands every nuance of the process? Or this could even be a task that only you use. This may determine how you present the steps within the task, and even what you write in the instructions. A task for the general public may need a longer instruction with more detail so that they better understand the input they need to provide, whereas the expert user may only need a few words of guidance because they may already understand what the input parameters are. And a task that only you will use might require just a one or two word prompt, or could even be written in Klingon.

Think of all of these things when designing your task, and document the design carefully and completely. Know how to set up the project file for this task, know every step that the task needs to include, and know what instruction you need to give the user to make sure that they can duplicate your designed outcome.

Tasks are extraordinarily difficult to build "on-the-fly" because if even one step is missed or configured incorrectly the entire process will fail. The more time you spend in this phase of development, the easier and more complete the task building process will be.

Components of a task

There are many different pieces in the task management environment, and it's important to understand what theyare and when they are used. A task is created from the Insert tab on the Ribbon menu.

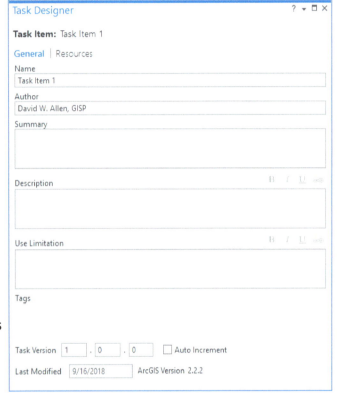

When the New Task Item button is clicked, the Task Designer pane opens. In this pane you will name the task, identify the author, and provide a summary, description,use limits, and tags for the task. *Note that the screenshots throughout this book will have the panes undockedfor clarity.*

Once this information is provided, a new folder is added to the Catalog pane that will contain all of your tasks. This folder will not exist until the first task is created but after that, new tasks can be created directly in this folder.

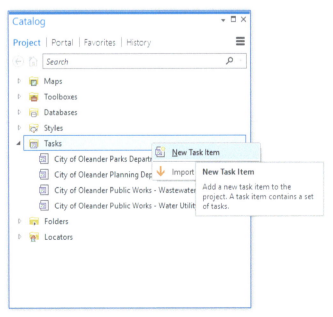

Note that this example contains four Task Items. Each of these Task Items can contain multiple tasks, and you can see that they are divided by department. A Task Item can contain multiple tasks, so all of the tasks developed for the water utility maintenance group are stored in the same place.

Storing tasks in separate items is also beneficial if, for instance, the water utility tasks for Public Works need to be shared with another user who does utility edits but doesn't do work for the Planning or Parks departments. The Task Item can be sent to an archive file, or packaged and e-mailed to a colleague.

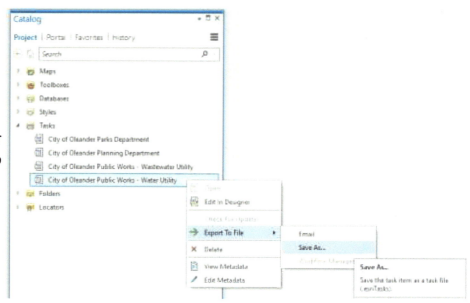

The creation process will open the Tasks pane. This pane will display all of the items included in the Task Item. In this example, there are two groups within the Tasks pane. One group holds the Task Items associated with creating new features, and one holds those associated with editing existing features. New Groups are added with the tool on themenu bar.

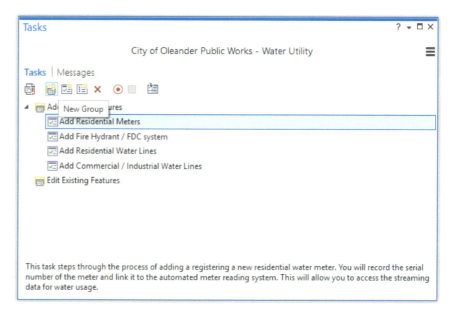

All of the components shown so far deal with organizing the task structure. The Tasks folder holds all the Task Items, and the Tasks pane shows the tasks and allows them to be grouped into categories. The Task Designer pane has been shown so far to allow the editing of metadata for the Task Item and the tasks, but it willplay an important part in the creation of the rest of the task components. Because of this, it is suggested thatyou dock the Tasks pane (which typically docks with the Contents pane) and Task Designer pane (which typically docks with the Catalog pane) into a single unit. The instructions on the following page will help you set up the editing and designing windows. Make sure you've downloaded the datasets for this book from

http://www.GisGuidebooks.com/Tasks

Setting up the docked panes

Undock both panes from their current locations. This can be done by clicking the arrow in the upper right of the box and selecting Float. Then drag the Task Designer pane onto the right side barof the Tasks pane docking manager.

Open the project *Task Pane Setup* and make this change to your project.

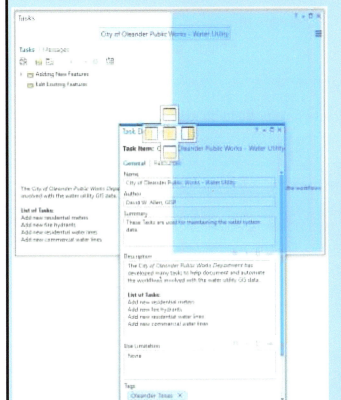

In the Catalog pane, find the Tasks folder, expand it, and find the Task Item 1 task.

Right-click it and select Edit in Designer.

Un-dock (float) both the Tasks and Tasks Designers panes.

When you drag one box to the center of the other box, the docking manager will appear. Dock the Task Designer pane to the tab on the right of the Tasks pane.

This is what the finished set of panes should look like, and this configuration is saved so that all future projects will have the panes docked correctly.

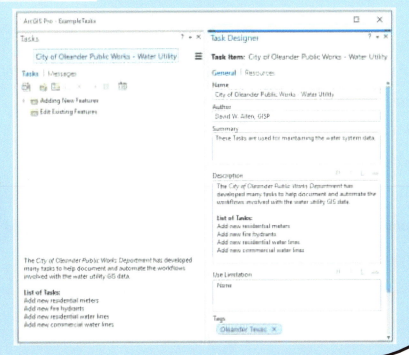

Once these panes are docked, you will move between them as a single unit while building and configuring a task, and close with a single mouse click when done. Conversely, you can reopen both windows in the same docked configuration by selecting Edit in Designer in the Task Item's context menu.

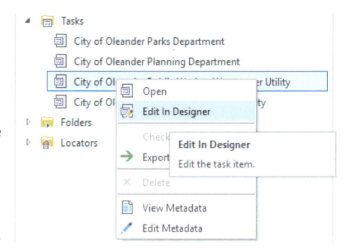

The task menu tools

There are several tools in the Tasks pane that are used to create new or build on existing tasks. They are shown here and described below. Refer back to this image for the location of the tools in future exercises and examples.

Validate – Highlight a task and verify that all steps within the task are configured correctly

New Group – Create a new group to help catalog your tasks

New Task – Creates a new task

New Step – Creates a new step in the highlighted task

Delete – Deletes a task, or a step in a task.

Record Commands – Highlight a task and record all keyboard, mouse, and tool actions into the task

Stop Recording – Stops a task recording session

Apply to View – transfers layer settings in a task to the active map view and Contents pane

That completes a review of the management components of a task. Once these components are designed and created, the rest of the work involves creating steps within the tasks, which is what the exercises will highlight. After this, only images referring to steps within a task will be shown, so you can reference back to these images and descriptions as you work through the book.

Steps in a task

Each task that you create will have steps, and as intuition would tell you these are the steps of the workflow that you would normally follow to complete a process. Each step is added, then configured to perform a process that may include clicking in the map frame, running a geoprocessing tool, setting a parameter, or providing a value needed for the next step. There are many parameters and options available for a step, and those will be explained and demonstrated throughout the course of this book.

To get an understanding of how steps are made and used, you will first look at a documented workflow, then run the task built from that workflow, and finally examine the steps in the task.

Before you begin the exercise it is important to note that is expected for you to already know how to use ArcGIS Pro. No instruction will be given on how to open project documents, how to access menu tools, how to configure layers and select features, how to search and run Geoprocessing tools, etc … If you are not comfortable working in ArcGIS Pro then it is suggested that you start with a book or class on that topic.

Exercise 1 – Examine a completed task

For this first exercise, you are the owner of a company that sells high definition TV antennas. As you may know, all broadcast television in the US can be picked up over the air in digital high definition, and the ETPH type antennas you sell are the best on the market. As a service to your customers, you want to provide a list of all the TV channels they can expect to receive with your top of the line antenna.

The workflow for this project is pretty simple. When a customer orders an antenna you geocode their address, identify where on the house the antenna will go, match it against the TV broadcast contour data, and export a table. The table is then e-mailed along with the customer's receipt. A more detailed workflow design – which was obtained by manually working through the process and writing down everything that was done looks like this (examine this written list of steps first, then on the next page you will open an exercise and go through the task step-by-step):

- Click the Locate tool in the Ribbon menu

- Type in the customer address – the map zooms to the location

- Open the Select by Location tool

- Set the Input Feature Layer to the TV Broadcast Contour data
- Set the Selecting Features to be a user drawn point

- Look for the house in the aerial photo and click on the roof to add the location
- Run the tool

- Zoom to the selected features

- Highlight the TV Broadcast Contour layer in the Contents pane
- Export the table by clicking Export Table (Data tab) and provide a location and name for the table

Export
Table

This is a straightforward workflow with tools you recognize, but when business is good you and your staff may be repeating this process 30 to 40 times a day. It makes sense to document this process and build it into a task so that any of your order takers can run the process and not have to wait on you, the GIS expert. The following instructions will have you run through this workflow manually to become familiar with the process.

1 **Open the Exercise 1 project from the provided materials**

When the project opens you will see the Esri World Imagery and World Boundaries and Places base maps, and the TV_Broadcast Contours layer from the Esri Living Atlas of the World. You will first want to test the workflow design manually to make sure that the design is both complete, and follows the correct sequence. Tip – try to use tools from either the Ribbon menu or the Geoprocessing pane and avoid using Context Menu tools. The Context Menu tools can be difficult (but not impossible) to add to a task. (remember that the Context Menu is the menu that opens when you right-click on an item).

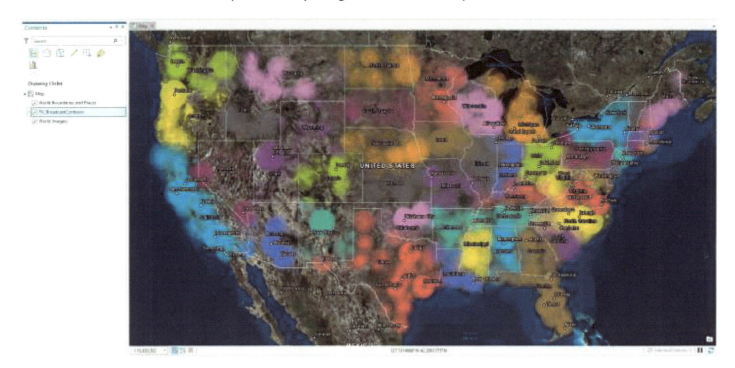

2 **Follow the listed workflow design on the previous page using the address of 600 W. 6th St, Roswell, NM, and place the selection point on the house at the southwest corner of the intersection. Name the output table using the customer name of Allie_N_Being and store it in the project's default geodatabase. The video Ex1_ManualProcess.WMV is included in the downloaded materials to demonstrate the process.**

Manual – User runs and user proceeds

This behavior requires that the user click the Run button to execute that actions for this step. When those actions are complete, the user must then click Next Step to proceed. This gives the user the most control over a step, but requires the most user interaction.

Auto Run – Step runs and user proceeds

With this behavior, the step will run automatically when it comes up in the task. It does, however, require user interaction to proceed to the next step. For instance if the action is for the user to interactively select some features in the map, then the Select Features tool could be run when the step starts. Once the tool runs the user can interact with the map to do manual selections, then click Next Step to proceed. This type of step behavior might also be used for an "information only"step that has no other action tied to it other than the documentation. For instance if part of the workflow was to burn the newly created data to a disk, you could add a step that simply displays the message "Put a blank DVD into the device", in effect pausing the task. The step would run, butwouldn't proceed until the user clicked and verified that a blank DVD was inserted.

Auto Proceed – User runs and step proceeds

This step behavior will wait for the user to run the action or tool, but when that action completes it will proceed to the next step without waiting for additional user interaction. This is the most common behavior used with geoprocessing tools. When the step is invoked the tools dialog is displayed. The user must fill out the parameters for the tool and click Run, but when the tool completes successfully the task will proceed to the next step without prompting the user. In the earlier example of creating a buffer, once the buffer is successfully created there's no need to ask the user if it's OK to go on since no addition interaction is needed for the buffer tool.

Automatic – Step runs and step proceeds

With this behavior the action for the step will be run with no user interaction, and when completed it will proceed to the next step automatically. This behavior is typically used for things like zooming and panning or going to the full extent, but may also be used on a geoprocessing tool if previous steps have created all the necessary requirements of the tool. For instance if step one creates a buffer and step two intersects the buffer with a predetermined, existing layer then the second step can be Automatic. No interaction is required. This behavior also has an option to hide it from the user. When a step is Hidden, the user will not see any dialogs associated with the step.

Optional – User can skip this step

As the name implies, the action for this type of step is totally optional. This step will stop and present an additional action to the user that is not required for the task to complete. For instance, you may stop and allow a layout to be exported to a PDF file before proceeding, and if that typeof file is not required at this time the user can skip the step and move on.

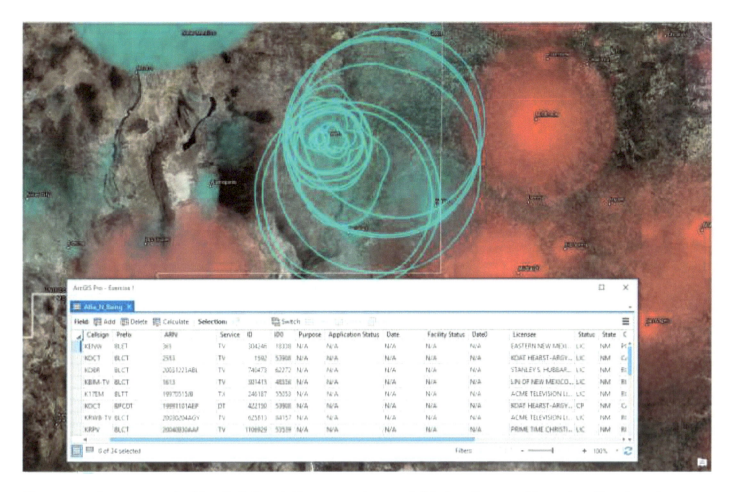

The output is a map and table of all the stations an antenna at this location would receive. Now imagine doing this 20 times a day, and then having to teach 20 other people to do this. Then all of you do this process repeatedly and you aren't allowed to ever make a mistake. It would make sense to build a task for this that will step users through the process perfectly every time.

Before trying to build this, it would be good to watch the task run first. A sample has been built in a fully manual mode so that you can see each step run. This means you will need to click both run (the Run button) and advance (the Next Step button) at each step.

3 Reset the map by clearing the selected features and zooming to the Fullview bookmark.

4 In the Catalog pane, expand the tasks folder to reveal the TV Broadcasts task. Double click to open the tasks pane.

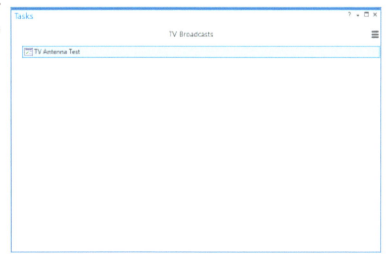

5 Double click the TV Broadcast Test task to open it. You can resize the Tasks pane so that you can see both the task running and the affect it has on the map.

6 The task process starts.

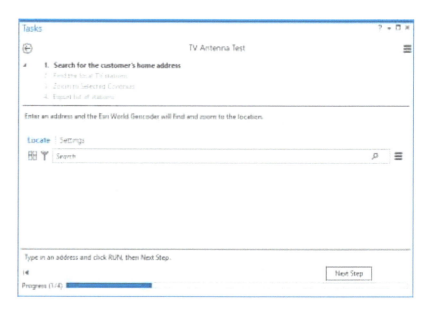

This Tasks pane will now take you through each of the steps in the workflow. The top part of the pane will show all the steps and which step you are currently on. Hint: you mayneed to click the arrow to expose this.

The middle part of the pane will display the actual tool being used, and any parameters that tool may need. Finally, the bottom part of the pane will display the step's controls and a progress slider. You will later see how to customize the instructions for each step, making it easy for novice users to understand the flow.

7 Enter the address of 18 Arco Iris Dr,

Roswell, NM. The Esri World Geocoder will display the matches - select the one that matches this address and the map will zoom in. Click Next Step.

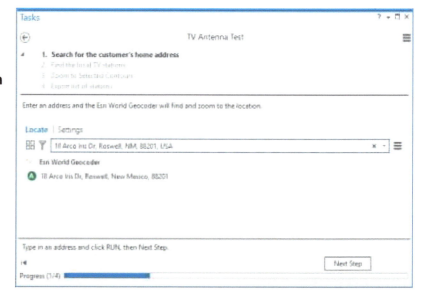

8 Set the Input Feature layer to TV Broadcast Contours and use the Point tool to show the proposed antenna location (in the middle of the roof). Click Run.

9 When the tool finishes the selection process, click Next Step.

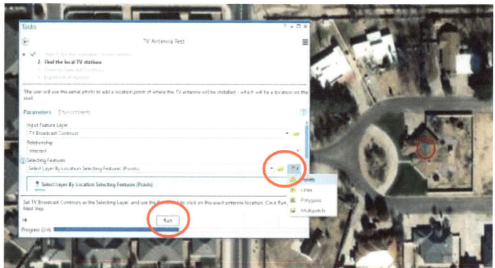

10 The Zoom to Selected Features tool requires no input. Click Run, and when it finishes click Next Step.

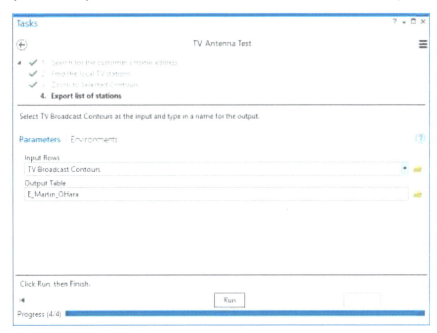

11 Set the Input Rows to TV Broadcast Contours and the Output table to E_Martin_OHara. Click Run.

12 This is the last step, so when it completes you will click Finish to close the task.

13 Close the Tasks pane and verify that the table was created in the project's geodatabase and that it contains the local TV stations.

14 Reset the map by clearing the selected features and zooming to the Fullview bookmark.

This sample task went through all the steps, but still required a lot of interaction from the user (clicking Run and Next on each step). This next part of the exercise will have you building this task, then later refining it to predefine some of the parameters and minimize user interaction on steps whose parameters don't change.

Creating a new task

To create a task, you always start with writing out and testing the workflow. Make sure that every step in the workflow is documented and have an idea of what instruction you would want to give the user as the go through your task. You already have a documented workflow for this process, and have even workedthrough it manually to make sure no steps were missed. It's time to create the task.

Exercise 2 – Creating a basic task

Earlier in this chapter you saw the components of a task and you will start by building this basic framework. Note that that since the Tasks folder already exists in the catalog pane, you have the option of creating the new task in one of two ways. You can go to the Insert tab on the Ribbon menu and click Task > New Task Item, or right click the Tasks folder to expose the Context menu and select New Task Item.

1 Open the Exercise 1 project (if you closed it after completing Exercise 1). Create a new Task Item by clicking Task > New Task Item on the Ribbon menu. The new Task Item will be added to the Task folder.

The docked Tasks pane and Task Designer pane should open together. If not, refer back to the instructions on how to set this up.

2 **Name the task "Dave's Antenna Emporium" and provide a summary and description. Since this is a Task Item and cancontain many tasks, it is a best practice tolist the tasks that you will include.**

Notice that as you fill out the information in the Task Designer pane, the name is updated in the Tasks pane. This will be true with each pane where you enter names and descriptions.

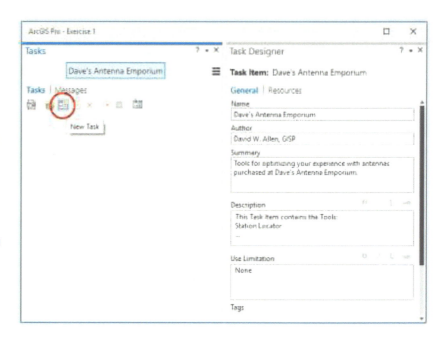

3 **In the Tasks pane on the left click New Task and name the new task "Station Locator".**

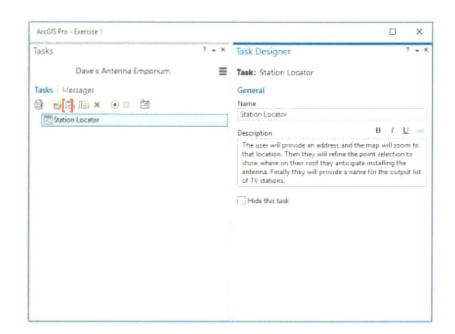

A new, empty task has been created. But at this point it doesn't do anything … there are no steps in it. There are two main ways to add steps to a task. The first is to use the Add Step button on the Tasks toolbar. This will add an empty step, and you will then configure the step and tie it to a tool or some process. While this is the more complex way of adding a step, you will find that in the long run it can be the fastest.

The second way, and the one which you will use in this example, is to start a recording session and work through the documented workflow manually. Each tool you use, whether it comes from a menu bar or the Geoprocessing pane, will be added to the task as a step. This will lay in a rough outline of tools that you will later come back and refine. Note that some tools may be added more than once when you both select a tool,then run it. Later you can refer back to your written workflow to decide which tools should remain in the taskand delete the rest.

The record process is started by clicking the Record Commands button, and ended by clicking the Stop Recording button. It's also important to note that actions such as moving between menu tabs, opening the Geoprocessing pane, or searching for a tool are not added as steps. A step won't be added until a functional tool is selected which allows you to dig into context menu or perform tool searches before any steps are added tothe task.

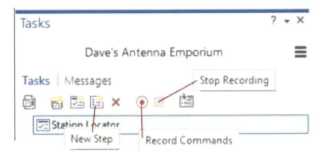

Review the detailed workflow for this task and decide what actual tools need to be run. Following the example task provided, the necessary tools are:

Locate (find the customer's address)

Locate

Select by Location (select the TV broadcast contours)

Select By Location

Zoom to Selected (zoom the map out to the selected features)

Export Table (create the output list)

Export Table

Remember that once you start a recording session, every tool or command you click will be added as a step in the task. Be careful not to mistakenly click too many extra tools. It's also important to execute the workflow as you go because some tools may not be available until the previous step is completed. For instance, the Zoom to Selection tool is not active until features have been selected, and you can't add an inactive tool to a task.

4 **Click Record Commands to start a recording session. Execute the workflow again using the parameters given above.**

5 **In the Map tab, click the Locate tool. Enter the address 18 Arco Iris Dr, Roswell, NM.**

6 **In the Map tab, click the Select by Location tool. Fill in the parameters as you did before, remembering to use the Point tool to identify the roof location. Click OK.**

7 **In the Map tab, click the Zoom to Selection tool. There are no parameters for this tool, but when you clicked it the tool was added to the task.**

8 **In the Data Tab, click the Export Table tool. Fill in the parameters and click OK. Then close the dialog.**

At this point you can click STOP RECORDING.

Notice that there are 5 steps, once for each tool you used in the process, but there were only 4 tools in the written steps. The Point step was added as part of the Select by Location tool when you marked the selection point. It will be removed later as you configure the task.

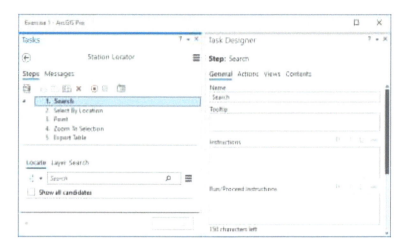

The task is saved as you go (no Save button) and if you executed this task as-is, it would certainly run but probably not give a very good user experience - there are no instructions with any of the steps. With some work, like adding documentation and refining the step behaviors, this can become a very user-fiendly tool.

9 **Highlight the first step in the task, called Search.**

The Task Designer pane will show the parameters that can be set for this step in the task. Note the four tabs of General, Actions, Views, and Contents. For now you will just work with the General tab, but later in the book you will set some of the more advanced parameters on the other tabs.

On the General tab you can see that there are several types of documentation that can be built for the step. The Name and Tooltip are quick references to what the tool does, and the Instructions and Run/Proceed Instructions can give the user more guidance on how they are expected to complete this step. These are fairlystraightforward, and you will have seen this type of information on almost every ArcGIS tool you have ever run so you should have an idea of what type of instructions are needed. Remember also that you need to be thinking of your audience and make the instructions appropriate for their skill level.

Below the documentation items is the Step Behavior selection. Within these behaviors, a step will Run or Proceed. Run means that the selectedtool or action will be started and will complete. For instance, if the action for a step is to create a buffer, then the step will present the Buffer dialog and wait for the user to enter the necessary parameters. When the user clicks Run, the buffer tool will execute and create the buffer. A message will appear showing that the tool has completed successfully. Proceed, or Next Step, means that the current step will be closed and the next step invoked with the behavior of that step controlling what happens next.

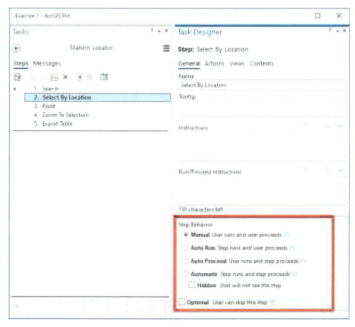

Now that you know what the step behaviors are, you can continue with creating your antenna task.

10 **With the Search step highlighted, provide appropriate documentation that will help the user understand what information they are expected to provide.**

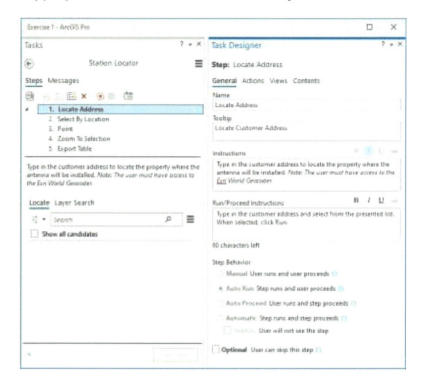

11 Note that the Step Behavior is automatically set. The Locate tool will always set itself to Auto Run.

12 **Click Step 2 - Select by Location. Rename the step 'Identify the Antenna Location' and provide appropriate documentation (see image below for suggestions).**

Next consider what step behavior you want to use here. The Select by Location tool will require the user to set some parameters, so it can't run automatically. When it completes, however, it doesn't need any addition user interaction before moving to the next step.

13 **Change the Step Behavior to Auto Run.**

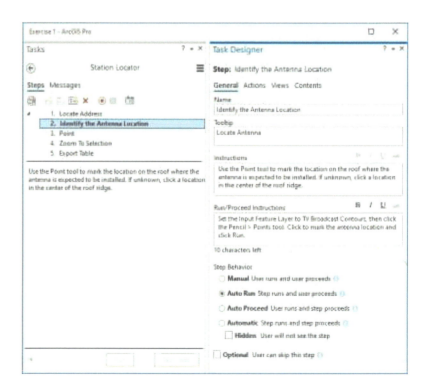

14 **Click Step 3 – Point. This step is a byproduct of the Select Layer By Location step and isn't needed. With it highlighted, click Delete.**

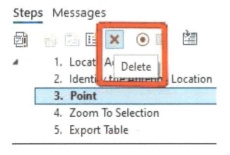

15 Click the new Step 3 – Zoom To Selection. Since this step requires no interaction, set it to Automatic with the Hidden option. It doesn't require documentation.

◉ **Automatic** Step runs and step proceeds ⓘ
☑ **Hidden** User will not see the step

Making this step hidden does two things. First it means that the step by default will run with no user interaction, and secondly it means that no feedback about this step is presented to the user. In fact, the user will notknow that this step exists or that any tools are being run. One consequence in making a step hidden is that steps with tools that take a long time to complete may cause the user to think the process has stopped or reached an error – and the user has no way of knowing what tool the task is using. In that instance it wouldbe a better user experience to not hide the step and add a note that the step may take several minutes to complete.

16 Tasks have no Save button, they are saved with the project. So now would be a good time to save your project.

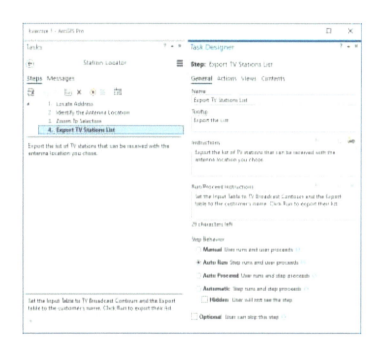

17 Finally add appropriate documentation for the Export Table step, which will export the selected records from the TV stations database toa new file.

18 Decide on your own if Manual is the best behavior for this step, or if you would like to use a different one.

19 Click the Back arrow to return to the Tasks pane, then close the dual window. Remember that tasks are saved as you go.

Tasks

⊕   Station Locator

Steps Messages

This completes the process of configuring all of the steps in this task. If done correctly, it should provide a nice and efficient user experience with no additional or omitted steps. Next you will test the task and see if it gives a smooth user experience. You should be familiar enough with the workflow to run through the task without detailed instruction, and understand when to go to the next step.

20 In the Catalog > Tasks folder, double click Dave's Antenna Emporium. Then in the Tasks pane either double click the Station Locator task or click the arrow at the right to open it.

21 Enter the address of Sapphire Dr & Onyx St, Roswell, NM.

22 Identify an antenna location on the house immediately west of the intersection.

23 Name the Output table Richard Solomon.

Your task should have completed correctly, and Dr. Solomon should now know what channels he can expect to get with his new ETPH Antenna. You may have also noticed that when you ran the task it only listed three steps. That's because the Zoom to Selection step is hidden. Notice also that the task progress indicator shows "Progress (1/3)" and moves through to "Progress (3/3)". Hidden steps don't even appear in the progress step count, which can make it confusing to the user if extra-long steps are hidden.

24 Export your task item to a file – right-click the task item and select "export to a file > save as" and store in the projects folder called "Antenna Task".

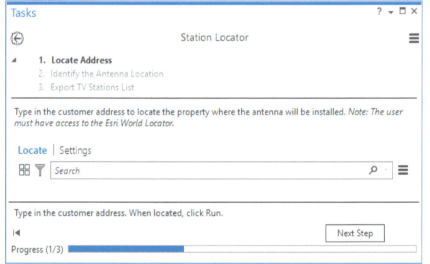

25 Save the project and if you are not continuing at this time, close the Exercise 1 project.

Two of the steps opened a separate geoprocessing tool dialog window and while this still works, it doesn't seem super friendly. Later you will see how to embed these windows in the main display of the task.

* Who recognized the names in this exercise? Allie N Being (alien being), E. Martin O'Hara (Uncle Martin from the 'My Favorite Martian' TV show) , and Richard Solomon (Dr. Solomon from the '3rd Rock from the Sun' TV show). And they all bought an ETPH (E.T. Phone Home) antenna made from an old Speak-N-Spell.

Rafael's Dilemma—FM transmission towers

This exercise can be worked using the materials provided with the Exercise 1 project file, or you may design and build your own task using these techniques on your own data.

In this scenario, you have a map with the locations of FM radio antennas as well as point features of all the cities in the US. Each antenna is owned by a radio broadcasting company and some of the companies own lots of these antennas. You will write a task that will find all of the antennas owned by a specified broadcast company, then use them to find what cities can be expected to hear their broadcast. It can be assumed that the FM signals will reach a distance of 60 miles. In the project is a table with a summary of antenna owners, and the top ten are shown here. For instance, CAPSTAR TX owns 299 antennas so running the workflow on their name should produce a list of at least 299 cities.

- First, open Exercise 1 if it is not already open and move to the FM Tower Locations map.

- Next, consider what the workflow for this scenario will be.

- Here's the expected workflow, but try writing your own first, then reference this list.

  - Choose a broadcast company licensee

  - Find all of the FM transmission towers that are owned by that company
  - Select all of the cities within 60 miles of the towers
  - Export a list of the city names

- Next, decide what menu buttons or tools are necessary to complete this workflow. Try working through this once manually and documenting the steps.

- Create a new task and use the Record Steps process to create the necessary steps in the task. Reference the documentation of the workflow that you made when manually performing the process.

- Configure the steps as needed and complete the creation of the task. You can try it out with one of the companies listed in the table.

Chapter 2 - Configuring Tasks

Exploring more task options

The last section had some really great techniques for building tasks, but there were some additional options that were not explored that can add even more automation to your processes. You were able to explore the General tab in the Task Designer fully. In addition to this tab is the Actions tab, the Views tab, and the Contents tab. Of these, the Actions tab can have the biggest impact on making a step easier to use and more intuitive for the user.

The parts of the Actions tab are the Command section, which will be examined first, and the Additional Actions section, which will be discussed later. The command section holds the tool thatwill be associated with this step, and which willrun when this step is executed. It has buttons that allow you to set, modify, or clear thecommand.

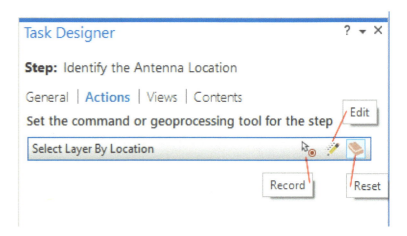

In the previous exercise you added commands to steps by recording a series of mouse clicks without accessing the Actions tab. When you use the Action tab you can define each command individually, and the first method for adding a command is with the *command* record button. The difference here is that this record button will only record one command for this single step, unlike the step record button that continuously added a new step for each command you clicked. This is particularly useful when the tool is from a user interface menu, such as a select or zoom tool.

The procedure is to first activate the command record tool, then click on the menu tool you want to add to the step. For instance, to add the Convert to Annotation command to a step, first click the command record button in the Action tab, then click the tool on the menu. Note that it's a good idea to activate the correct part of the menuand locate the desired tool before starting the record process. Otherwise you may accidently click on somethings else and the wrong command might get recorded.

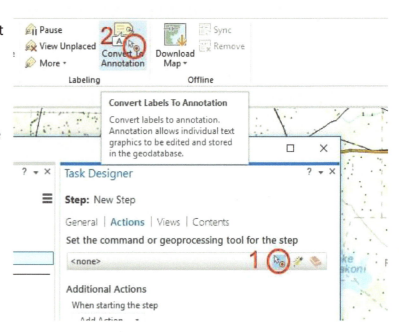

The record button also works on context menu items. For instance, if you wanted to include a command that would zoom to the extents of one of the layers in the Contents pane you would clickthe command record tool, right click the layer to expose the context menu, then click the desired command. In this example, the Zoom to Layercommand is being added to a step. Note that when using the record tool the cursor changes toan arrow with a record symbol.

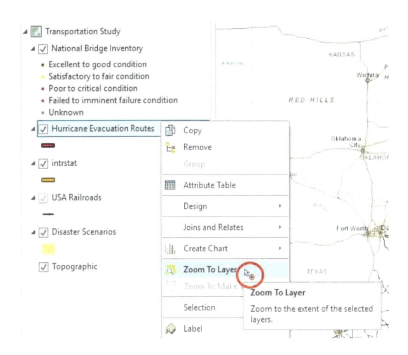

Next, the Edit button serves two purposes. It can be used to configure a command or menu tool added with the command record button, or it can be used to add a command or geoprocessing tool from a pick list. If no tool is currently added to the step, the edit button will present a choice of which type item to add.

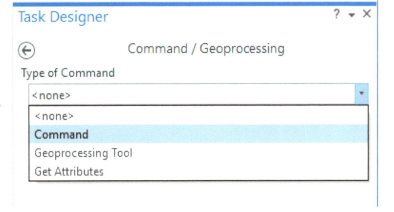

The Command choice will open a searchable dialog box with which you may find a menu command. Practically every button click from every possible menu is represented here. The drawback is that selecting menu tools which are removed from their menu context may leave you guessing if the tool will perform the correct task. For instance, searching for Zoom returns multiple pages of zoom tools with no idea of the exact differences between them. It is probably better to use the command record tool if you arewanting to add a command from a specific menu.

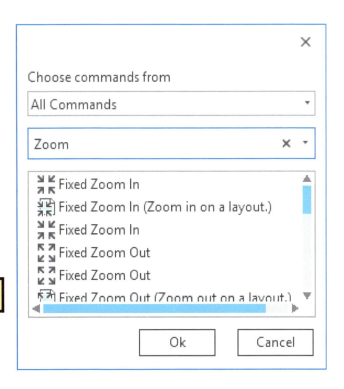

Rafael's Question—When will the search be valuable?

When you are searching for either a very unique tool or a custom tool, model, or script that you have written.

The Geoprocessing Tool choice will open a dialog similar to the regular Analysis > Geoprocessing pane and allow you to search for any geoprocessing tool. In this example, searching for Select Layer will return a list of familiar geoprocessing tools that can be researched in the help to determine exactly what they will do. Custom tools, models, and scripts may also be registered and searched for as a geoprocessing tool.

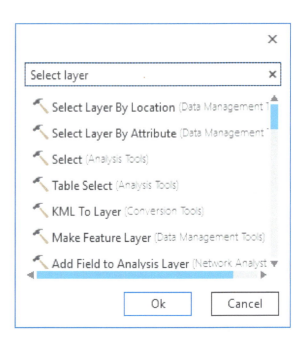

Configuring Actions

Once a selection is made, the parameters for the selected tool will be displayed. Menu tools like Export,

Select, or Zoom typically don't have any parameters to set and you are finished. But geoprocessing tools willhave a dialog to configure, exactly as if you had run the tool from the Geoprocessing pane. Any parameter left blank will need to be filled in by the user when the stepis executed, but it is also possible to preconfigure the step by adding values to some of the parameters.

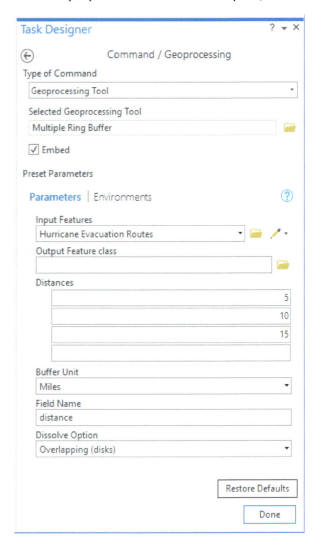

For instance in this sample workflow, the user selects a featurein the previous step, then this step will create multiple buffer rings. Note that the input feature class, buffer distances, and other parameters are preset so that the user must only providea name for the output file. Just remember to click Done so thatthe settings are stored. Note the Embed option. When checkedthis will cause the dialog for the tool to be displayed in the Taskpane rather than being displayed in a pop-up window as they were in the TV antenna task you built.

The final choice of the edit button is the Get Attributes command. More will be discussed later in this book about using and configuring this command.

Setting Additional Actions

That concludes a description of the first half of the Actions pane, so now it's time to turn your attention to the second half of the pane.

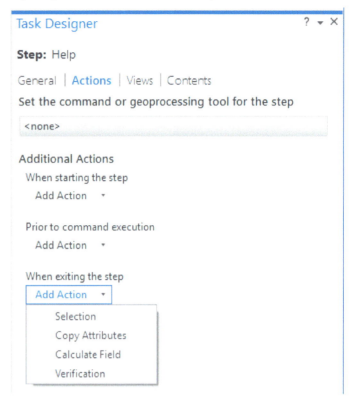

This part of the pane is called the Additional Actions section and allows you to perform a limited action either before, during, or after a step. You can even configure multiple actions on a single step.

The actions available are to perform a feature selection,copy attributes from a field, calculate a value into a field, or verify that an action meets a certain selection criteria. These can get very complex, so it's important to know your process completely and use that to guideyour settings here.

The Selection actions fall into four categories, the first of which is to save features to a selection set for use within the task. The features to save may be the current selected set, all the features that were created so far in this task, or all the records that were modified so far in this task. Then at any time you can configure a step to retrieve the stored selected set. For example, in the previous task you could save all the broadcast contours into a set for use later.

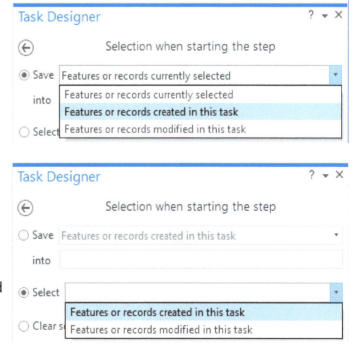

Another option is to create a set from new features created within the step. As an example, you may create a task that lets a user trace building footprints,one by one, on top of an aerial photograph. Then when they are done all the newly created items from the step can be saved into a temporary set. If you thenneeded to perform an action several steps later on all of the new buildings they could be retrieved from this set. Note that this set only persists within the task and once the task is completed it goes away.

The next action is to select all the features that have just been created or modified in this task. The selected set can then be used in the current step. For instance you may have edited the attributes of 30 features in the previous step, then want to select them all and create a buffer.

Next, a simple function: Clear the selected features. This will start the step with no features selected. There's not a whole lot to say about this other than it's great insurance against accidentally applying a geoprocessing tool to features that you didn't know were selected. As a best practice, it good to use this for any step where you will be creating a new feature selection set.

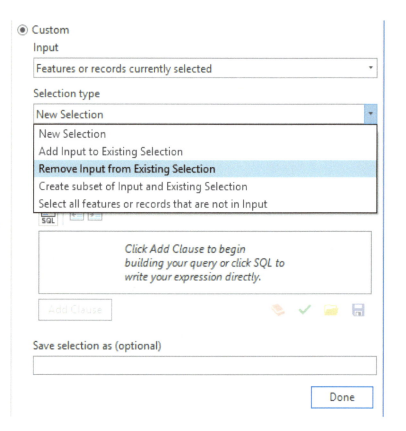

And the final option is to create a custom selection. This is very similar to the tool Select Layer by Location with the input being features currently selected, created, or modified in this task. The selection types are also similar to ones presented in the Select Layer by Attribute geoprocessing task. These include creating a new selection, adding or subtracting from the currently selected features, creating a subset of the selected features, or reversing the selected set.

Once a selection method is determined, you can add a optional filter layer or selection expression. The selection query is built with the standard expression builder seen in many other tools. In this example, paved hurricane routes are removed from the current selection so the step will act only upon the unpaved roads. Examine the parameters shown here to see how this action is configured. There's even an option to save the selection to a new location.

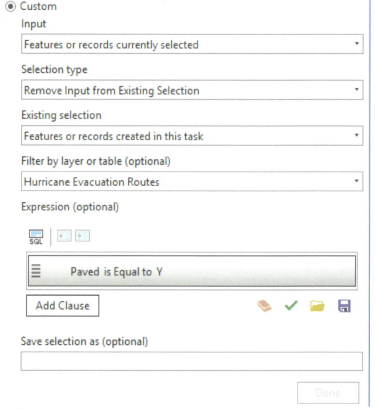

24

Another available action is to copy an attribute to be used later. This attribute can be copied from the currently selected features, features created in this task, or features modified in this task - the same choices asthe selection actions. Once an input table is identified, the Add Attribute button is used to set up the copy action. Any named attribute can be copied into a variable.

For instance you may want to copy the road name of the currently selected feature into a variable that can be used to populate a field later in this step. Note that multiple fields can be copied into variables, however these variable can only be used within the task and dissipate when the task is done. You'll learn how to use these variables later.

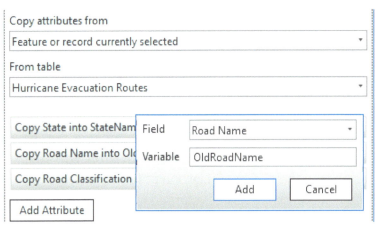

The last action that can be performed before the step begins is to calculate a field. This uses the standard field calculator interface, but remember that the calculation is done only on the features that you identify as selected, created, or modified in this task.

Remember that these pre-action tools are designed to work only in the task, and only on features you specify. If you need a more global actionyou will set that as a command or geoprocessing tool.

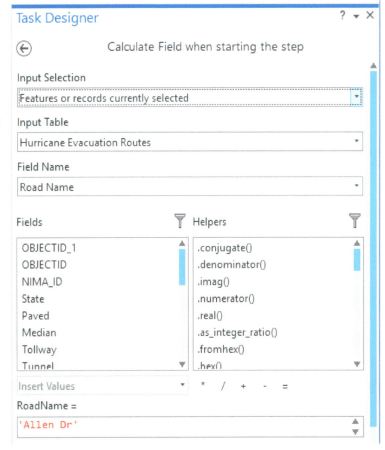

Rafael's Question—how do I know when to use the Additional Actions?

Well the Clear Selection action can be used at the start of any selection step. After that, look at your workflow diagram and see if there are any steps that might only need to be done on features associated with thistask. They might be ones you just created or modified, or ones that you picked up in a selection process.

The same actions can be configured to occur prior to the command in the step executing, or when the command in the step has completed and the task is moving to the next step. You will need to examine your workflow to decide when the additional actions should be invoked.

One additional option is available for these last two actions, and that is to add a verification function. This verification process is designed to checkand make sure that the correct number of features is selected before the step moves on. For instance, if the previous selection of finding only unpaved hurricane routes returned no records, you would want the task to stop rather than try to process an empty selection. As you can see, itis possible to set up a very detailed verification query.

Note that if the condition of the verification is not met, the task quits rather unceremoniously and no more steps can be run, so it's not a great way to control a common user error.

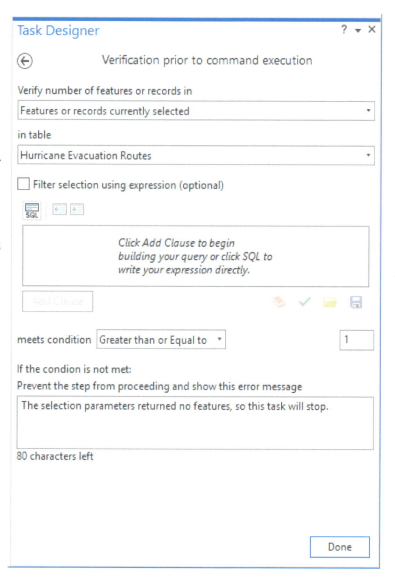

That's a fairly comprehensive tour of the settings available on the Actions tab. You may want to spend time learning the nuances of these settings and learn how they can be used together for best effect, and the exercise will demonstrate some of these step configurations are not meant to be a programming language.

However, the ability to store values into variables and make a decision on stopping the task are verypowerful controls. The Views and Contents tabs of the Task Designer pane will be discussed later.

This scenario has you being the GIS expert for a state and regional planning commission. Every other year they are required to build a Threat Against Transportation (TAT) report showing what damages may occur to critical transportation infrastructure in the event of a natural disaster or human created disaster event. The threat may cause the transportation network to be out of service for some time, and portions may even be rendered unusable in the long term. The planners have a formula to figure out the monetary loss, but for each disaster scenario they want you to provide certain summaries of the features. They will plan a disaster scenario and draw a polygon on a map showing the affected area. You will then take that polygon and find the length of rail line passing through this polygon and the length of Interstate Highway or major trucking routes that pass through this polygon. They have planned out dozens of scenarios, but for each report you will only run 5 or 6, depending on the particular response capabilities they want to highlight.

This sounds like a complicated workflow, and it's important that every time you run through this the results are based on the same process. Plus the process has to be repeatable, not just for the many times you'll run it this year but in two years you will run through more of the scenarios with updated data using the same process. The results must be consistent and it may be difficult to remember all the steps two years from now. They may also run it periodically to help plan the next TAT report and decide what scenarios to include. You could be running this thing six to eight times every few months, so this is a perfect time to build a task.

1) **Open the Exercise 3 project file and review the layers it contains.**

You will see the polygon layer for Disaster Scenarios. These are the ones that the planning board drew out for you to use. The state-wide plan has 175 scenarios to study, but for this example only 10 are provided. The attributes for this layer have fields for each of the totals that you will be discovering.

The other datasets are from the Esri Living Atlas of the World. The data includes a single line representation of the USA Railroads as well as the USA Freeway System. The process only calls for a total length of these that pass through the disaster zone, so the attributes are unimportant.

The first part of the task creation process is to write out all the steps in the workflow and determine what tools may be necessary. There may also be an instance to use some of the new action tools you learned about, so pencil those in as a suggestion. You can determine later if they are necessary, and if so where in the Additional Actions they should fall.

2) **Write your own workflow and check it against the one shown on the next page. If you are working in a classroom environment, have the class discuss and design the workflow.**

Rafael's Question—How do I get started designing the workflow?

First decide what the outcome needs to be, then look at the data you have. The final result for this task will be the length in miles of railroad that fall within the disaster polygon. You have the polygon and the lines representing railroads. Now think of what functions you will need to apply to the railroad lines to get the desired end result. Is it a clip, intersect, union, or something else. You may need to list possible tools and read the help file for each tool to make sure you are using the best one. What about working with tables? Again, see what tools are available and read the help to choose the right one. Take good notes, change themif needed, and don't be afraid to try some of the tools on a test dataset before deciding on the final process.

The workflow below is the one being demonstrated in the numbered steps. If you have a completely different workflow in mind, work through this one first with the instructions, then design and build a task for your workflow and compare.

⇒ Clear the selection

⇒ Select a Disaster Scenario polygon.

⇒ Make note of the scenario name and unique ID number from the fields Disaster Name and Scenario Number.

⇒ Use the selected polygon to clip out the railroad lines that pass through it.

⇒ Recalculate the railroad line lengths in miles (shape_length is in the wrong units)

⇒ Perform a summarize function to get the total length of railroad.

⇒ Add the total length to the field Rail Length.

⇒ Reselect the Disaster Scenario polygon if necessary.

⇒ Use the selected polygon to clip out the highway lines that pass through it.

⇒ Recalculate the line lengths in miles (shape_length is in the wrong units)

⇒ Perform a summarize function to get the total length of road.

⇒ Add the total length to the field Interstate Length

⇒ Finish (perform any cleanup or file closeouts)

The workflow above needs to be reduced to a list of the tools and commands necessary to complete the processes. This will equate to the number of steps needed in the new task.

3 **Move the map display to the bookmark Scenario 1, then perform the entire workflow and write down all the tools you use. Make a note of parameters for the tools and any results that may be important when you build the task. Complete your list first then compare to the list below. If in a classroom situation, discuss the list before proceeding.**

There are many menu item commands and geoprocessing tools in this workflow. This list also contains suggestions of Additional Actions that may be done in the task.

Select Feature

This is the Select Feature command from the Ribbon menu

Have the task clear selected features before starting

* The user will manually select a feature in the map

Clip (Analysis tools)

USA Railroads

Output Feature Class is Railroads_Clipped

Calculate Geometry

Recalculate the Miles field in the correct units

Summary Statistics (Analysis Tools)

Railroad length

Output Table is Railroad_Summary

Calculate Field

Store the results of the summary tool in the Rail Length field of the Disaster Scenarios layer.

The process repeats for the highways.

    Clip (Analysis tools)
        USA Freeway System
        Output Feature Class is Highway_Clipped
    Calculate Geometry
        Recalculate the Length in Miles field in the correct units
    Summary Statistics (Analysis Tools)
        Highway length
        Output Table is Highway_Summary
        Calculate Field
        Store the results of the summary tool in the Interstate Length field of the Disaster Scenarios layer.

It looks like this task could have close to 10 steps, so it will take good attention to detail to get everything set and configured correctly. In the previous exercises you made the task using the record tool, which is certainly a viable way to add tools and create steps. But in this exercise all of the steps will be created and configured manually so that you will gain some experience using these interfaces.

Start with creating a new Task Item, and a new task.

4 **Return to the bookmark Scenario 1 if necessary.**

5 **On the Insert tab, click Task > New Task Item. Name it "Disaster Analysis" and give it an appropriate summary, description, and tags.**

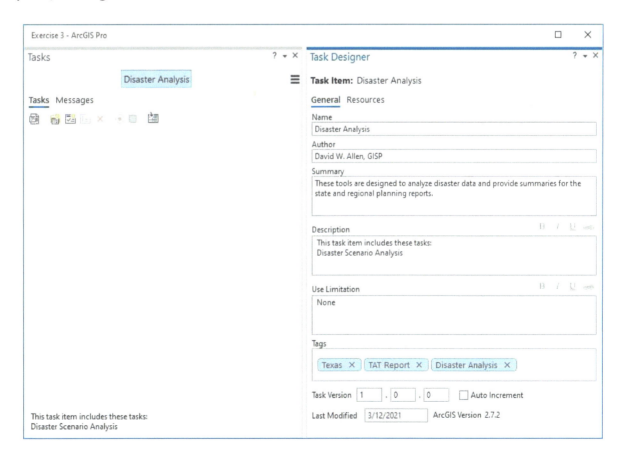

6 In the Tasks pane, create a new task called Disaster Scenario Analysis.

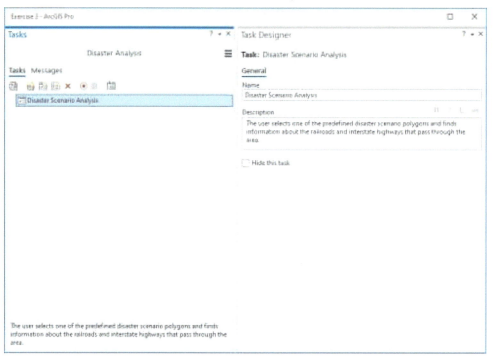

7 Click New Step and name it Select Disaster Polygon. Provide a tooltip and instructions as shown.

What should the Step Behavior be? You will want the Select tool to activate, then have the user click the Next Step button when the selection has been made. This is the Auto Run behavior.

8 Set the Step Behavior to Auto Run.

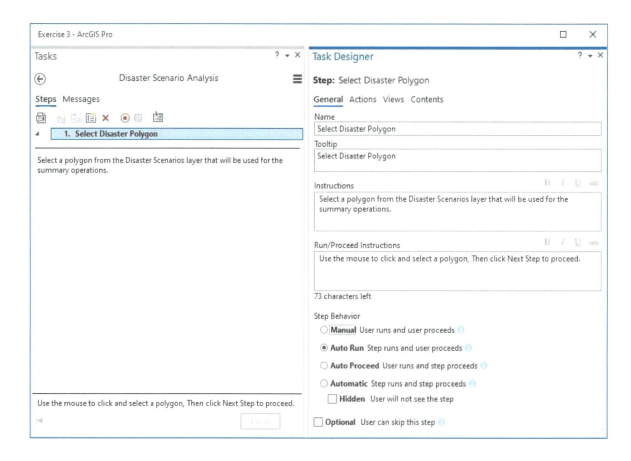

9 Click the Actions tab. Make sure the Map tab is active in the Ribbon menu.

10 In the command line, click the Record button, then click Select > Rectangle on the menu. You can click the Edit button to see the options for this command if you like, but the Select by Rectangle tool has no parameters.

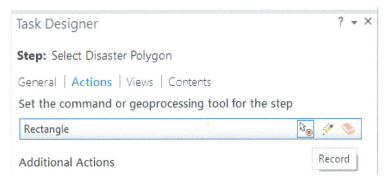

In the workflow, it mentions that the task should start with no features selected. One way to do that would be to clear the selected features manually, but remember that one of the Additional Actions under "When starting the step" is to control selections. Setting that here will ensure that the task always starts with an empty selection.

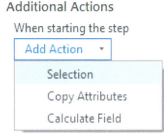

11 Under "When starting the step", click the Add Action drop down arrow and select Selection. The Selection pane will open.

12 Click the Clear Selection button, then click Done to save the action.

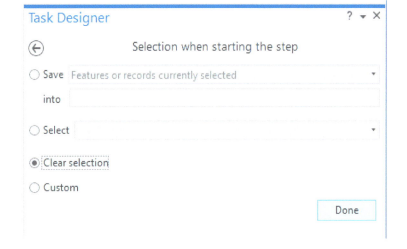

There's another action that might be interesting to try. During the course of this step it may be necessary to change the selection to features other than the Disaster Scenario polygon. This might be to perform a function or to copy attribute values into a field. When the next part of the process gets back to needing the Disaster Polygon selected, you don't want to make the user select it again. So it will be helpful to store the selected feature into a temporary selection set for future reference. If you recall, there's an Additional Action that will let you store a selected set of features and recall them later when necessary. That will prove to be very valuable here.

13 Click the Add Action button under "When exiting the step" and select Selection.

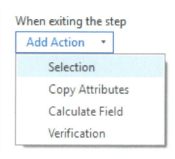

14 Set the "Save" setting to "Features or records currently selected", and the "Into" to DisasterPolygon.

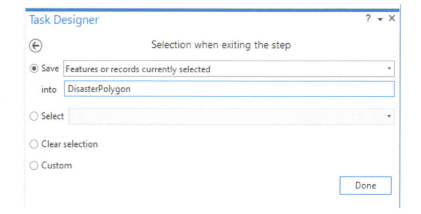

15 Click Done to return to the Actions tab.

Note that added action at the bottom of the Actions tab.

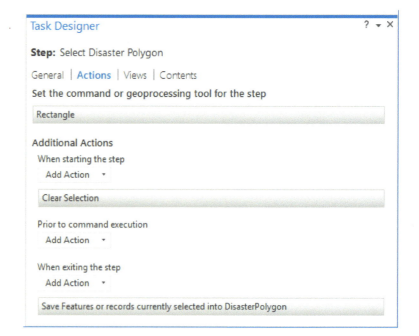

That's a busy step! In one process this step will clear the selected features, allow the user to select a disaster polygon feature, and create a temporary selection set. How many mouse clicks is that saving?

The next command will be to run the Clip tool. This will always use the same input files of USA Railroads and Disaster Scenarios. The currently selected polygon will be the only feature used for the clip. The output file will be a temporary name that will get overwritten each time the task is run. As you build this, see how many of these parameters can be preset.

16 In the Tasks pane, click New Step.

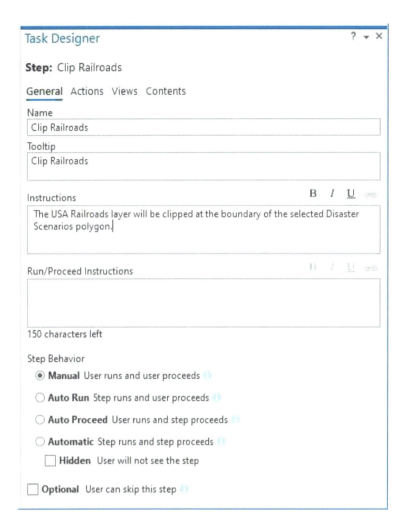

17 Provide a name of Clip Railroads, and add appropriate tooltip and instructions.

What do you think the Step Behavior should be? The clip tool will open and not require any user interaction to run. After it runs, it should automatically move on to the next step. That would be the Automatic behavior. Now consider if you would like this step to be hidden. Depending on the size of the polygon and the number of railroadlines that cross through it, the step may take a while to complete. So even though the step will start and finish on its own, you will probably wantthe user to be aware that this step is running.

18 Set the Step Behavior to Automatic.

What will the Actions be for this step? It will run the Clip command and you can preset some of the inputs for that, but it won't have to deal with any selections or attributes either before, during, or after the step completes.

19 Click the Actions tab. Then select the Analysis tab on the main Ribbon menu.

20 Click the Record button in the command line of the Actions pane, then click the Clip tool in the menu.

> Note: It will open the Clip tool, but you should close it. That is not where you configure the action.

21 Click the Edit button on the Actions tab command line to open the Clip tool configuration screen.

22 Set the Input Features to USA Railroads, the Clip Features to Disaster Scenarios, and the Output Feature Class to "Railroads_Clipped" in the project's local geodatabase.

23 Review the settings for the Clip tool. When you have verified all the parameters, click Done.

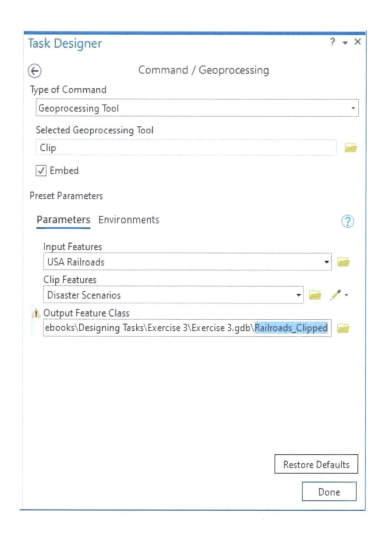

The output layer will have a field called Miles to show length, but since it is not a system field it won't automatically update. You will need to recalculate that field to get the correct mileage. This is done with the Calculate Geometry Attribute tool from the geoprocessing menu.

24 Add a new step called Calculate Geometry Field. Provide a tooltip and

25 description. Set the step to be Automatic.

The command for this step will be added by opening a tool search window and finding the Calculate Geometry Attributes tool.

26 Move to the Actions tab. Click the Edit button to open the Command / Geoprocessing pane.

27 Set the Type of Command to Geoprocessing tool.

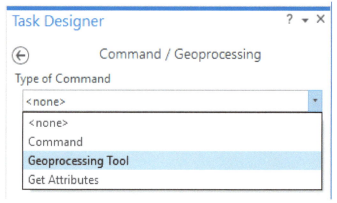

28 A tool selection pane will open. Use it to find and select the Calculate Geometry Attributes tool, and click Ok.

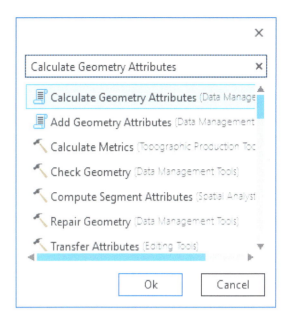

29 Set the Input Features to Railroads_Clipped and the Target Field to Miles. Then set the Property to Length and the Length Units to Miles.

The Railroads_Clipped layer should exist as a result of your checking the process manually. If that layer is not there, go back and run through the steps to create these layers.

30 Click Done to return to the Actions tab.

The next step for the railroad features is to run a summary statistics and get the total length of the lines that were clipped out. When it is done, the output file will have a field called SUM_Miles containing the total length of the lines. This should be stored in a variable for use in the next step where you write the value into the Disaster Scenario feature class.

31 Add a new step called Railroad Summary and give it an appropriate tooltip and instructions.

32 Decide what the Step Behavior should be (Hint: There are no user parameters to set) and set it.

The command for this step will be added by opening a tool search window and finding the Summary Statistics tool.

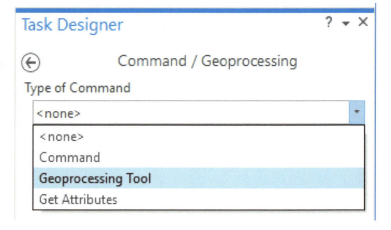

33 Move to the Actions tab. Click the Edit button to open the Command / Geoprocessing pane.

34 Set the Type of Command to Geoprocessing Tool.

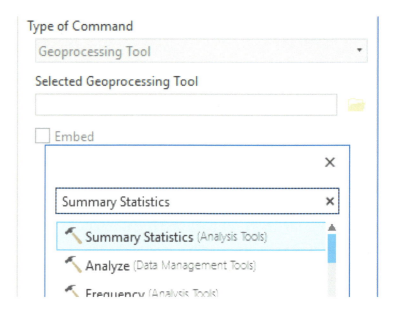

35 A tool selection pane will open. Use it to find the Summary Statistics tool, and click Ok.

36 In the Preset Parameters area, set the Input Table to Railroads_Clipped. Then set the Output Table to be "Railroads_Summary".

Next is to set up a summary statistic to run. Since you have recalculated the Miles field to have correct measurements, you will do the summary on that field.

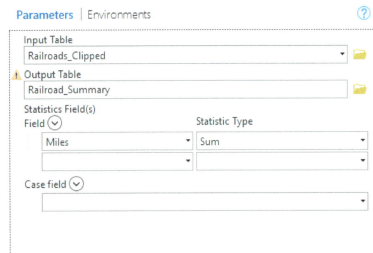

 **Set the field to Miles and the Statistic Type to Sum.**

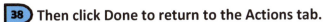 **Then click Done to return to the Actions tab.**

When the command completes it will have made a field called SUM_Miles which will contain the total length of lines. The goal is to take that value and transfer it to the Disaster Scenarios polygon layer into the field Rail Length.

This can be done in tasks, but it's a little trickier than a programming language command might be. You have to first select the single record in the summary table, then make an attribute pairing with a variable name. This will create a task variable containing the summary value which will persist as long as the task is active. Then you have to select the target feature, and in this case it's the disaster scenario polygon, and use the Additional Actions option of Calculate Field with the temporary variable to transfer the value. This will add two new steps to your task:

⇒ Select the record in the summary table / make the variable and store the value
⇒ Select the Disaster Scenario polygon / calculate the value into the field.

> *Rafael's Question – Can you use the Additional Action Selection in the "When exiting the step" to set a selection for "Features or records created in this step"?*

Unfortunately you can't. As far as the task is concerned you didn't create records here, you created a table. If you had used a tool to add records into an existing table, then the Additional Action Selection would work.

39 Add a new step and call it SelectSummary. It will be Automatic so it doesn't really need a tooltip or instructions. Would it be acceptable to make this step hidden?

40 On the Actions tab, set the command to Select Layer by Attribute (you can choose whichever method you like to use to get this tool).

41 Set the Input Rows to Railroad_Summary and the Selection Type to New selection. Leave the rest blank and click Done.

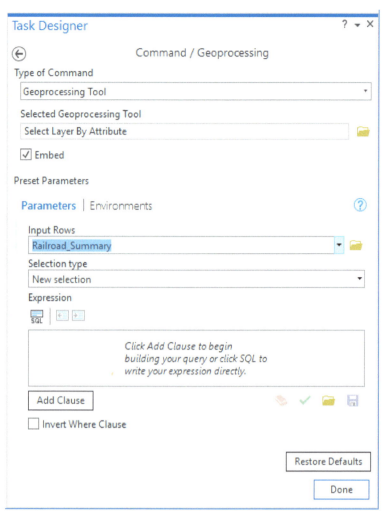

Note that a selection with no expression will return all of the records in the table. Since this table will only ever have one record, the summary data, the task has selected the record with the total length of railroads.

42 Add an Additional Action under "When exiting the step" and select Copy Attributes.

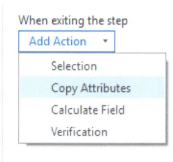

43 Set the "Copy attributes from" value to "Feature or record currently selected" and the "From table" to Railroads_Summary. Then click the Add Attribute button.

44 Add a field / variable pairing to store the Railroad_Summary field value in a variable called RailroadLength. Click Add to make the pairing.

45 Click Done to finish configuring the step.

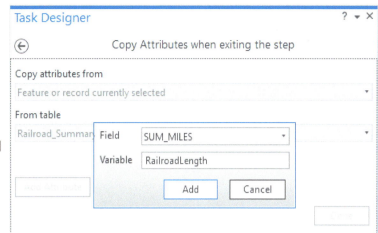

Phew - another busy step. But since it was selecting features it has probably cleared the selected feature in the Disaster Scenarios layer. Luckily you saved the set and can retrieve it easily.

46 Add a new step called Select Disaster Polygon – it will be Automatic so it doesn't require instructions. Again consider if this step could be hidden.

47 Move to the Actions tab. Add an action under "When starting the step" to be Selection.

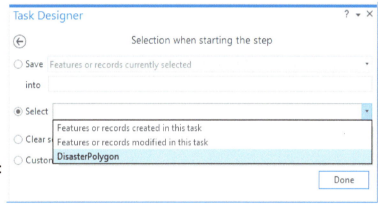

48 Click Select, and in the drop down box select DisasterPolygon. Click Done to finish.

This premade selection was the one you saved back on Step 1. The step will have no tools or commands associated with it, but it will use the Additional Action feature Calculate Field. This will perform basically the same thing as the geoprocessing tool Calculate Field but with one very important distinction … the geoprocessing tool can't access the task variable that you just set up. It can only be accessed by an Additional Action function.

Hiding a step removes it from the step counter when the task is run. So if you have a task with 9 steps and three are hidden, the step counter will display Step 1 of 6. The step counter also display a progress bar so that you can see how long steps take to run. If you had a very compute intensive step that took a long time tocomplete, and you make it hidden, the user will not see a progress bar for the step. They may, after waiting aperiod of time, think that the task has frozen and take steps to interrupt it—when in fact it may be doing exactly what you planned. If that step were visible (and even if it's automatic) you can have the step display a message saying "This will take a while", plus the user will see the progress bar.

49 Under "When exiting the step" click Add Action and select Calculate Field. Set the Input Selection to "Features or records currently selected", the Input Table to Disaster Scenarios, and the Field Name to Rail_Lengt.

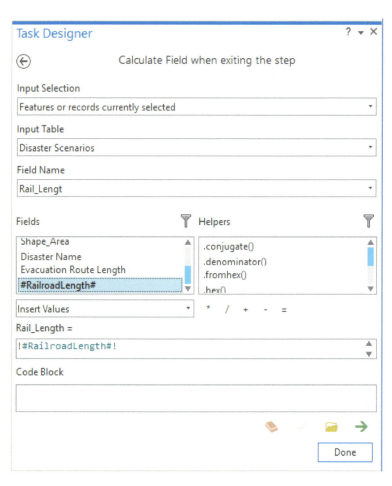

50 In the Fields list, scroll down to the bottom and find #RailroadLength#. Double click it to add it to the calculation.

Did you figure out that #RailroadLength# is thetemporary variable you set up in this task?
Rafael did!

51 Click Done to complete the setup.

Since the last two steps were automatic, it would be nice to drop in an informational step letting the user know that things are still OK and give them the opportunity to cancel if things are going wrong. This next step will have no action associated with it, just a message stating that the railroad length summary has completed. Then the user will need to click a button to proceed. This will be an Auto Run step.

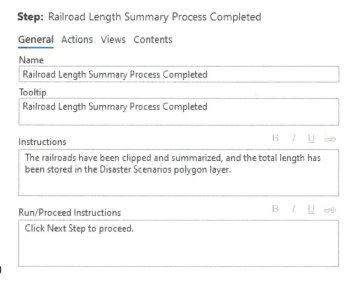

52 Add a new step called "Railroad Length Summary Process Completed". Provide an informative message about the completion of the step with instructions to click Next Step to proceed.

53 Set the step behavior to AutoRun.

54 Click the Back arrow in the Tasks pane to return to the Task Item list, then close the pane.

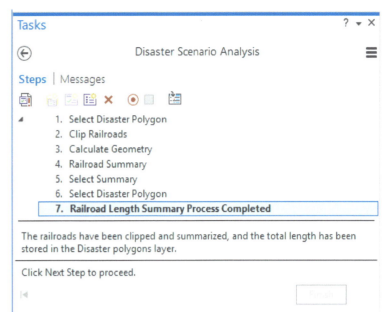

Testing Your Task

That completes the configuration of the first part of the analysis, so now would be a good time to test and troubleshoot the task. If any issues arise, it will be easy to identify where they are occurring and fix them rather than wait until the entire (and very complex) task is completed.

Exercise 4 – Test and modify the Disaster Analysis task

1 Move to Bookmark 1. Double click the Disaster Analysis task Item in the Catalog pane, then double click the Disaster Scenario Analysis task in the Tasks pane. Follow the instructions as if you were the user.

2 When it finishes, close the Task pane.

3 The results should be that the value is now written into the correct field in the attribute table. Open the attribute table for the Disaster Scenarios layer, review the value, then close the table.

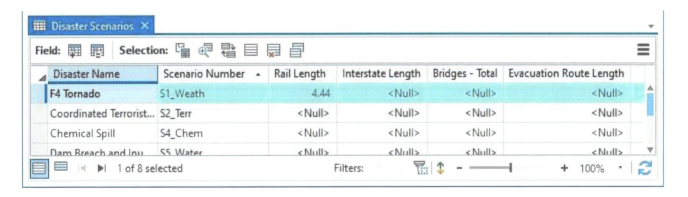

The task worked rather well, but others who have tested it have raised some concerns. The first worry is that some users were selecting random features that were not part of the Disaster Scenario layer. If the user selected a highway feature, for instance, the task would fail when it tried to run the clip command. Others were trying to advance from the first step without selecting a feature causing the task to perform actions on the entire dataset rather than just a single selected feature. The planners were also reporting that some of the totals were very high, indicating that the user had selected more than one scenario polygon at a time. There needs to be some safeguards built in to better control the selections that the user will make.

The Task Designer pane has two additional tabs that haven't been explored yet, and that is where to look for one of the answers. The first is the Views tab which lists all of the maps and views in the project. This example has multiple map and layout views in the list.

You can set which maps, scenes, or layoutsare open for a particular step, and in whichof these the actions will take place – the active pane. When the step begins, the settings are changed for this step, which may include closing items from the previous step. The settings can be copied from the previous step, changed to match the current project view, or set independent ofboth these. In the example above, the Active view is the map Exercise 5-5a. At the same time, the map Exercise 5-5B and the layout Tutorial 5-5 are also open. Work canbe done across all of these views. And when this step starts it will close the map Exercise 5-4 and layout Tutorial 5-4. This can help prevent the user from accidentlyworking in the wrong view.

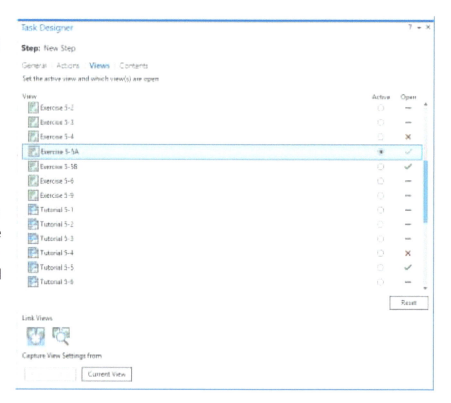

And finally, the Contents tab. In this pane you can control the settings for visibility, selectability, editing state, snapping, table selectability, and labeling. You can leave them as-is in the current view, or turn them on or off to override the current view. Note at the bottom of the pane is the option to control the snapping type (point, end, vertex, edge, etc...), which would come into play when you are adding new features.

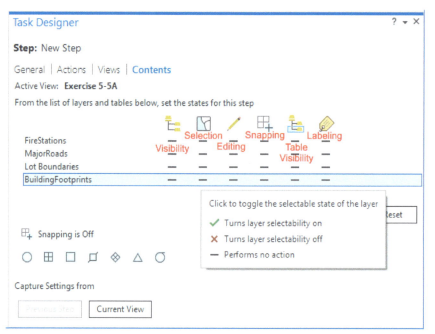

You can see that controlling the views for each step in the task can be critical when dealing with a project that has many maps and layouts. Some tools aren't available in a layout that are available in a map, and setting this will control which tools are available. This also gives you the ultimate control over the editing environment with the Contents settings. Remember that the more guidance you can give the user the better chance they will be successful with your task.

The project for the task you are building only has one view, so that won't stop users from selecting the wrong features but setting the Contents controls will. You want to make the Disaster Scenarios layer the only one selectable – and there's a nice shortcut for this.

4 Open the Task Designer pane with your task displaying all the steps.

5 Highlight Step 1 and go to the Contents pane.

6 Right click the Disaster Scenario layer and select Only make this > Selectable.

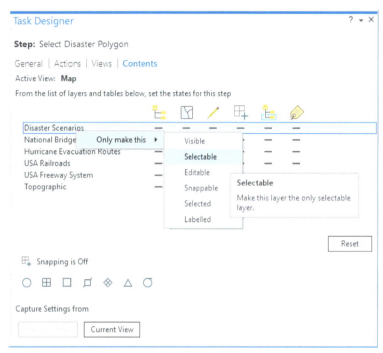

The resulting settings will look like this:

Note that the settings for all the layers was changed. Even if you are going to have several layers selectable, it's a good practice to use this tool to basically "clear the board" before setting up your custom configuration.

That solves the problem of selecting the wrong features, but what if they don't select a feature ... or select too many features? This task is designed to perform analysis on one feature at a time, and if you selected more than one disaster polygon the results would be wrong. There's an Additional Action function that will solve this called Verification. It can check the selected set against a parameter set by you and stop the task if necessary.

7 Move to the Actions tab, keeping Step 1 selected.

8 Under "When exiting the step" click Add Action and select Verification.

In the Verification pane, build the sentence: "Verify number of features or records in <u>Features or records currently selected</u> in table <u>Disaster Scenarios</u> meets the condition <u>Equal to 1</u>.

9 Add an error message to the user, and click Done to save the settings.

Adding these additional controls and safeguards should keep users from making critical mistakes when running your task.

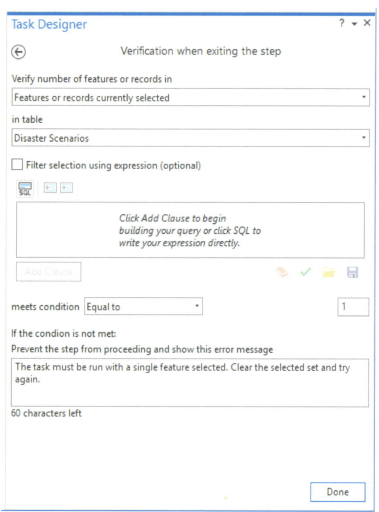

Task Designer ? ▾ ✕

Verification when exiting the step

Verify number of features or records in

Features or records currently selected ▾

in table

Disaster Scenarios ▾

☐ Filter selection using expression (optional)

Click Add Clause to begin building your query or click SQL to write your expression directly.

Add Clause

meets condition Equal to ▾   1

If the condion is not met:

Prevent the step from proceeding and show this error message

The task must be run with a single feature selected. Clear the selected set and try again.

60 characters left

Done

Extending Your Task

The next bit of data to add to the analysis is to get the length of the highways that run through the disaster scenario polygon. The process will be exactly the same as the one you built for railroads with the only changes being the input data and the field where the results will be stored. These are the steps you will repeat butwith the highway data.

2. **Clip Railroads**
3. Calculate Geometry
4. Railroad Summary
5. Select Summary
6. Select Disaster Polygon
7. Railroad Length Summary Process Completed

A lot of work went into creating and configuring the steps so far, and here's the really excellent news. You can copy and paste steps! To repeat this entire process with another dataset will involve copying a step, changing a few of the configurations, and moving on. The step behaviors and actions will be the same.

Exercise 5 – Setting additional task actions

1 Open the Tasks / Task Designer combination pane, if necessary.

2 Right-click step 2, Clip Railroads, and select Copy. Right-click step 7 and select Paste.

3 Update the Name and Instructions for the new Step 8 on the General tab and replace "Railroads" with "Highways". Note that the name of the step will change automatically.

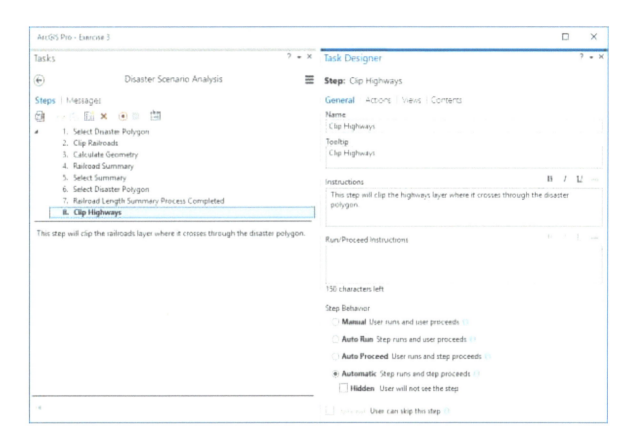

4 Move to the Actions tab.

The only action for this step is the Clip tool. You will need to reconfigure this for the USA Freeway System layer. The instructions here are going to be a little more concise since you should be familiar with all these processes.

5 Click the Edit button on the command line (Clip Tool).

6 In the Preset Parameters area, change the Input Features to the USA Freeway System layer. Then change the Output Feature Class name to Highways_Clipped.

7 When the changes have been made, click Done.

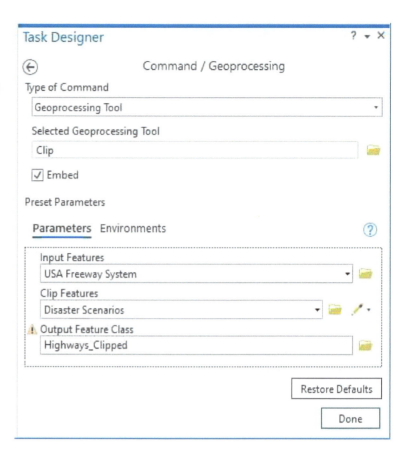

The next step to copy is the step that calculates the length of the clipped features using the Calculate Geometry Attributes tool. The copy process will place the right action in this step, you just need to reconfigure it.

8 Return to the General tab. Copy Step 3 and paste it after step 8. Update the Name and Instructions as before to reflect the Highways layer.

9 Move to the Actions tab and click the Edit button. Change the Input Features to Highways_Clipped and the Target Field to Length inMiles with the Property of Length.

10 Click Done.

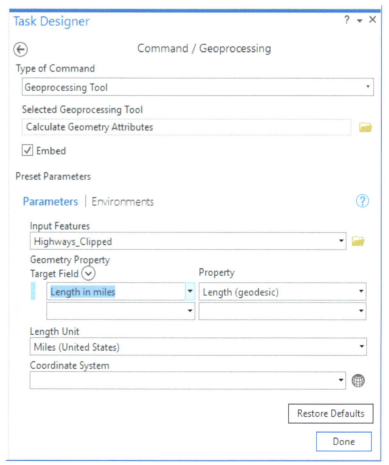

Continue with the step that creates the summary table.

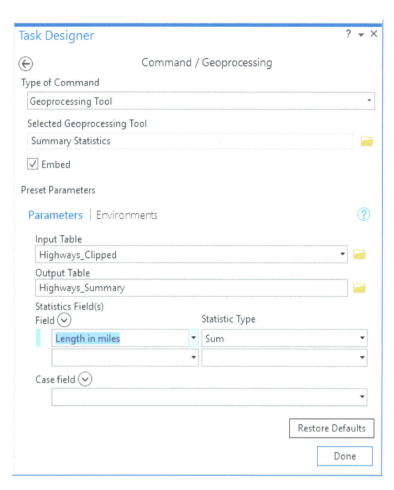

 **Return to the General tab. Copy Step 4 and paste it after step 9. Update the Name and Instructions as before to reflect the Highways layer.**

12 **Move to the Actions tab and click the Edit button. Change the Input table to Highways_Clipped and the Output Table to Highways_Summary.**

13 **Change the Field to Length in Miles and the Statistics Type to Sum.**

14 **Click Done.**

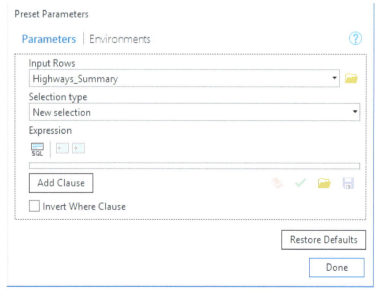

 **Copy Step 5 and paste it after Step 10. The information on the General tab doesn't need updating, but the Actions tab will have two areas to change.**

16 **Click the Edit button in the command line and change the Input Rows to Highways_Summary.**

17 **Click Done.**

Remember that the purpose of that step was to select all of the records in the table, and running the Select Layer by Attribute tool without a query will select all of the records.

There's also an Additional Action under the "When exiting the step" area to update. It will need to be updated to use the Highways_Summary table and put the total lengths of highways into a variable called HighwayLength.

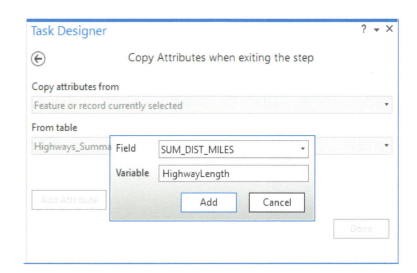

18 Click the Edit button on the Additional Action line. Change the From table to Highways_Summary. The existing attribute action will be deleted.

19 Click Add Attribute and set the Field to SUM_DIST_MILES, and the Variable to HighwayLength. Click Add, then Done.

This has saved the desired value into a variable, and now you must save this into the Interstate_Length field in the Disaster Scenarios layer. The step that did this for the railroad data had no tools associated with its action but it does have two Additional Actions. The first action is to select the disaster scenario polygon again, and that won't change. The second is to copy the attribute from the previous step, and that will need to be modified.

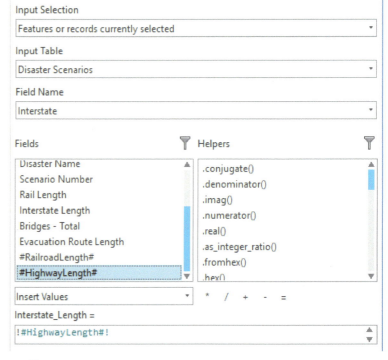

20 Copy Step 6 and paste it after Step 11. Click the Edit button for the second action. Change the Field Name to Interstate, then scroll down and select the #HighwayLength# variable for thefield calculation.

21 When completed, click Done.

You added a notification step after doing the calculations for the evacuation routes, and you should add one here, too. Remember that it had no actions associated with it and exists only to let the user know that things are progressing smoothly.

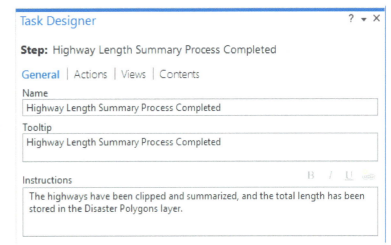

22 Copy step 7 and paste after Step 12.

23 Modify the name and instructions to reflect the highways layer. Then return to the Task pane and close the paired windows.

The task got pretty big, but when you break down the steps you can see that it's just a lot of simple, easy to understand steps strung together. This will be the case with most tasks.

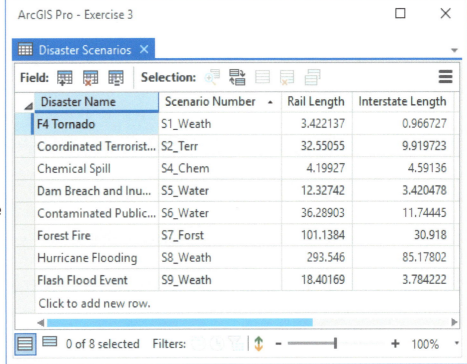

24 Zoom to several of the bookmarked scenarios and try running the task for each of them.

25 Close any dialog boxes that are open and save the project. Remember that tasks are saved as you build them, then stored with the project file.

That task was quite involved and moved through a lot of the capabilities and options that are available in tasks. One of the important parts of designing the task was to decide when to use the Additional Action settings. Since these are unique to tasks and work slightly differently than a normal programming language, interjecting these to your task can take some thought. But the benefits are great. Storing the selected feature in the first step was wise because it allowed you to regain that selection at any time. Transferring the values from summary tables to the selected disaster scenario polygon was also a unique challenge. It would take fewer actions to do this manually, or even in a model or script, however within the task it additional steps. In the end this was inconsequential because the steps run in automatic mode without user interaction and they'll hardly know anything is happening. Did you set any of your steps to be hidden? If so, can you justify that action? There were also some progress notification steps added that didn't really do anything, they just let the user know if things were moving along correctly. These are nice when you are debugging a task but in reality you could take these out or make them automatic so that they can deliver their message but not require user interaction in the task.

Rafael's Dilemma—Refine the task

Before moving on to a new scenario, it might be interesting to re-examine the actions of the TV antenna scenario and see if you can add some additional tweaks to make it run smoother.

Open your completed Exercise 1, find the Dave's TV Emporium task, and open it in the dual Tasks / Task Designer pane. The following are settings that you may want to consider adding:

- Select the second step (Identify the Antenna Location) and move to the Actions tab.

- (See note below) Preset the Input Feature layer to TV Broadcast Contours.

- Make the command Embedded.

- Add an addition action to clear the selected features before the step executes.

- Select the fourth step (Export TV Stations List) and move to the Actions tab.

- (See note below) Preset the name of the Input Rows table to TV Broadcast Contours.

- Make the command Embedded

- Set a verification action to make sure that there is at least one feature selected prior to the command executing.

IMPORTANT NOTE: Esri changed the way menu interface buttons call geoprocessing tools so that they will run faster - these are tools selected from the Ribbon toolbar rather than the Geoprocessing pane. Consequently a command added to a task from the menu cannot be edited. To accomplish two of the suggestions above you will have to delete the recorded menu selection command and add it back by searching the geoprocessing tools for the tool of the same name, then configure it. The command can then also be embedded.

Try running through the task with these modifications and see if the changes made it any easier or faster. If you can think of other modifications to make, try them out.

Chapter 3—Combining Advanced Task Techniques

Throughout the other exercises you have seen many different techniques used in tasks. These included basic ones like the setting the step behavior and adding command actions. You also performed more complex techniques like adding additional actions, recording steps and commands, and using task variables to store selected features. And finally you used some of the more advanced techniques like copy/pasting steps, controlling the views and contents, setting validation steps, transferring attribute values between steps, and more. As you continue the next chapter you will bring all these techniques together to make very powerful tasks. Using these techniques helps you control what the user sees and does, but still allows the flexibility the user needs to perform the work.

Exercise 6 – Feature interaction

This exercise will provide more of an opportunity for you to manage user interaction, although it doesn't add any new techniques. The scenario is that the Code Enforcement offices in the small Texas town of Oleander have come to you with a project. They are having to start a new swimming pool inspection program where they need an inventory of pools, with addresses, so that they can schedule visits to each pool. They will be looking for pools that are not being maintained, and they will check that the pools have a working pump and proper chlorination equipment. Plus they'll want a measurement of the surface area of each pool because that factors in to some of their ratings and calculations. The bad news is that there is currently no pool inventory data. Someone will have to create it.

1 **Open Exercise 4 and zoom to the Area 1 bookmark to get a view of the available data.**

The three inspectors have each selected a subdivision where they will be working (the three areas are bookmarked), and these pools will need to be added to the inventory first. You don't want to get bogged down creating the pool inventory for the entire city so you will propose this workflow in which the inspectors will draw in the new pool polygons themselves:

⇒ The inspectors will zoom to the subdivision where they will be working and pan across the properties looking for pools
⇒ When a pool is found, they will trace the outline of the water
⇒ They will continue panning around until several pools are found and traced that would represent one day's inspections.
⇒ They can then take a list of the pools to inspect into the field and perform inspections.

They'll be another aspect of this workflow where their tablets show the pools to inspect, but that'll go through other processes that don't involve this task.

With this workflow, the inspectors will build the pool inventory themselves in a just-in-time manner and building a task will help streamline the work of drawing them. The pool inventory will need to have the address, which is in the parcels layer, so that will need to be transferred to the final inventory. As far as the GISwork involved, the workflow looks like this:

⇒ The inspector draws a polygon around one or more pools in the PoolSketches layer
⇒ The PoolSketches layer is intersected with the Parcels layer to get the address

⇒ The area in square feet will already be in the shape_area field

⇒ The final step is to add all the new pools to the Swimming Pool Inventory layer.

2 **Review the workflow and datasets and design a task to accomplish this, writing out the process and steps (don't start creating it yet). Be specific in what steps you will include, what each action the step will perform, and note the use of any Additional Action functions.**

3 **When you are finished, compare it with the outline below. If yours differs significantly, build both.**

Rafael says "Don't peek – write your own first".

Step 1 – Draw new pools

⇒ Step behavior is Auto Run

⇒ Actions – Set command to Create features (Embed the tool)

⇒ Additional Actions – Select Features or records created in this step

⇒ Additional Actions – When exiting the step, save all features created in the step to a variable called NewPoolsDrawn

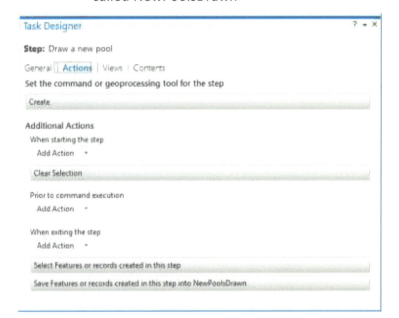

⇒ Views - Set the current Map as active

⇒ Contents - Make the New Pool Sketches the only layer that is selectable, editable, or snappable. (Hint – right click the layer and use the context menu)

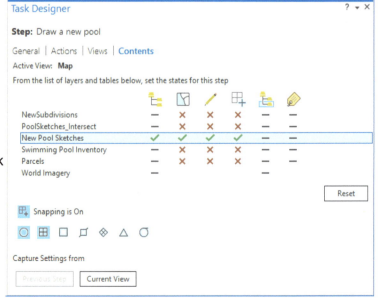

Step 2 – Save the pool sketches

⇒ Step behavior is Automatic

⇒ Actions – Set the command to Save

⇒ Additional Actions – Save all

⇒ Views – Reset all parameters

Step 3 – Intersect pools with parcels

⇒ Step behavior is Automatic

⇒ Actions – Set command to the geoprocessing tool Intersect

* Intersect New Pool Sketches with Parcels

* Output file is PoolSketches_Intersect

⇒ Additional Actions – When starting the step select the features in NewPoolsDrawn

Step 4 – Append new pools to inventory layer

⇒ Step behavior is Automatic

⇒ Actions – Append using a field map

* UseCode = UseCode
* Prop_Add = Prop_Add
* EKEY = TAXID

* SurfaceArea = Shape_Area

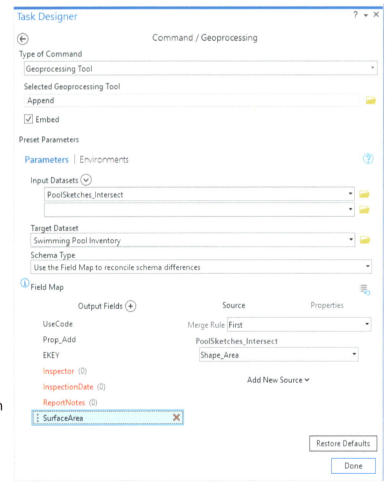

Step 5 – Finished

⇒ Message that task has completed

⇒ Step behavior is Auto Run

Remember that the "wrap-up: step is totally optional. Here it it used just as a note to the user that things have completed successfully, but even without this step the user will have a "Finish" button.

You now have an idea of the workflow and what steps you will want to make—and even an idea of the tools and actions for each step. If your design differs significantly from the one provided, build this design first before attempting to build your version.

4 Create a new Task Item called Inspector tools.

5 Use the steps above (or your own design) to build a new task called Draw New Pools.

Here's an idea of the steps that you will create. If you have an issues creating or configuring a task, review the instructions from the other exercises for help.

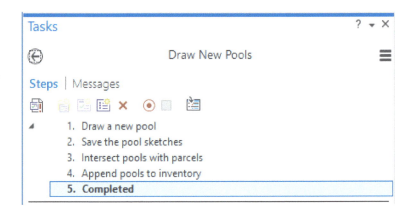

When the task is complete, you will want to give it a try before turning it over to the inspectors.

- This task sounds really complicated, but it's really only 4 steps (plus the "You're Done" note at the end. Take your time and go through the configurations for each step carefully and it's a breeze.
- The best Create Features tool for drawing swimming pools is the 'freehand' tool. If you give the inspectors a choice of tools, they may not figure this out. But the Draw Freehand tool isn't a Geoprocessing tool so you can't search for it. Instead, open the Create Features dialog, click on the New Pool Sketches layer to open the list of tools, then use the Command Record button to click on and record the Freehand tool.

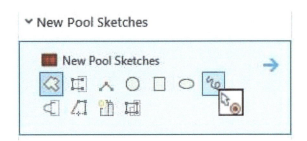

- Make sure that the New Pool Sketches is the only layer that can be selected, edited, or snapped by configuring the Contents tab.
- For Step 2 you can use the Command Record to save the tool from the Edit menu.
- For steps 3 and 4, don't try to record these from the menu, make the Geoprocessing tools and search for them in the list. Otherwise you can't embed them and make the Automatic.
- I made steps 2 through 4 automatic but only hid step 2. The other steps take time to complete and I'm afraid users might think the process is hung without a status indicator.

Chapter 4 - Combining Tasks and Models

Introduction To Models

As you read at the start of chapter 1, there are both similarities and differences between tasks and models and the trick to using them in your workflows is determine when it is best to use one over the other. The choice might be easier if the workflow requires a process that only one of them can do, but sometimes it's a judgement call as to which would work best.

To help you decide, you first need to understand what models can do. A model is a framework in which you can string together geoprocessing tools. The output of one tool may be used as the input for another tool, and this creates a linear workflow. Models run in a totally automated environment. Once you start a model it will run uninterrupted until it finishes. Other features of models include the ability to create and work with variables; iterate through a selected set of features, files, or an entire workspace; use decision making toolsto branch a workflow based on some parameter; and even incorporate Python scripts for really advanced routines. Plus there are 'model only' tools that are only available inside of a model. These include commands that can pull values from an attribute table or even logical statements that can add a decision making capability.

But there are some drawbacks to models. First, the processes must be run in a linear fashion and cannot skip a step, which you know a task can do. Models also don't have the ability to accept user interaction – the user must have setup or selected all of the features the model will act upon BEFORE running the model. And the menu tools that are available to tasks aren't available to models. Models can only run geoprocessing tools and model only commands.

You may also find that some parts of your workflow may be done with a task just as easily as it could be done with a model. For instance, running through several geoprocessing tools that don't require user interaction could be done with either a task or a model. The task may have the tools all preconfigured and run as hidden steps. There is nothing wrong with that, although it may require some extra steps to get output values from one tool to the next. But a single model can include many geoprocessing tools and it not only excels at passing values from one tool to the next, it has a lower processing overhead since it doesn't have to manipulate any user interfaces like a task does … and thus it will run faster. To the user going through the workflow therewould appear to be no difference – except that the model would run faster.

As you gain more experience with models you may find many scenarios where it is beneficial to use a model and incorporate it into a task. Again, the user experience doesn't change. The task can move into the model, finish, and come back without the user realizing that they were handed off to another item.

Anatomy of a Model

Within a model is of course a geoprocessing tool, symbolized with a yellow rectangle. The tool will have input variables (blue ovals) and output variables (green ovals). Sometimes models will have one or more of the input variables marked as an input parameter, noted by having a small P next to the blue oval. This means that the user must supply a value for this variable when the model is run. In this example, the input variable is also a model parameter meaning that the user will have to navigate to and select the input files. The output variable could also be a model parameter, meaning the user could name the output file rather than use a default value.

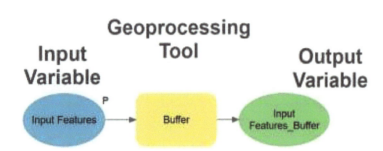

In models, the ovals always represent 'variables' which can be preset or configured for the user to define. All other shapesare tools that will perform some function.

To string multiple tools together, an output variable is used as an input variable for the next tool. Note in this example how the output of the first tool is linked to the second tool. It becomes the input and a new output is generated.

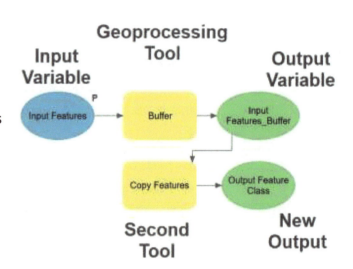

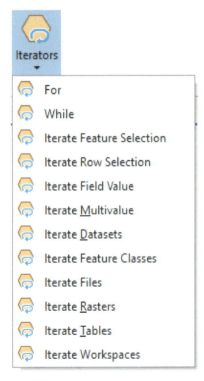

These geoprocessing tools can then be combined with other features of models to perform very complex functions. The first of these special functions are called Iterators. If you are familiar with programming terms, you may already know what an iterator is. This is a function thatwill step through the input data one piece at a time, perform an actionon that piece, then move to the next piece. You can see in the image below that you can iterate through just about any component of a dataset. Notice also that there are two conditional iterators. The For iterator will iterate through the data until a specific condition is found, and the While iterator will iterate through the data until a specific conditionis met. You can read the help for a more detailed explanation.

Next are the Utilities functions. These can be used to manipulate values within the attributes of the feature classes or tables that the model is processing. The two most commonly used, as you might expect, are Get FieldValue and Calculate Field Value. They do exactly what their names imply and give you the ability to work with fields and their values directly.

- Calculate Value
- Collect Values
- Get Field Value
- Parse Path
- Select Data

And finally, probably the most powerful aspect of models are the Logical statements. In programming terms, logic is the ability to determine what something is and act in a specific fashion based on the discovery. For instance, you might use the Get Field Value tool from the utilities functionsto extract the value of the Gender field from a feature class. The value is either M (male) or F (female) but how does the model know? It can't look at the value with its eyes and determine what it is with its brain. Butyou can use the "If Field Value is" function in the model to define two actions – one for the value M and one for the value F. In this image you can see more of the logic tools used for decision making.

- If Data Exists
- If Field Exists
- If Selection Exists
- If Coordinate System Is
- If Data Type Is
- If Feature Type Is
- If Field Value Is
- If Row Count Is
- If Spatial Relationship Is
- If Value Is

- Merge Branch
- Stop

By using these special 'model only' functions you can add true programming features to your model – and in fact ModelBuilder is often described as a visual programming interface for ArcGIS. This only scratches the surface of what ModelBuilder and models can do, so if you find this intriguing you could find a good book on ModelBuiler or try some of the online training classes for ModelBuilder.

Calling A Simple Model

You saw in the sample model that a model can have an input parameter that the user must define before the model can run. We also know that any geoprocessing tool, when run, will act only upon on the features or records that are selected. Therefore if a task is used to select several features, then a geoprocessing model will only act upon the features that are currently selected and not the entire dataset.

Exercise 7 – Calling a Model From a Task

For this scenario, the city planner has written a model that will draw a 300' buffer around any buildings that are selected. The buffer is always drawn around the buildings, and is always 300'. The only input that the model needs is the name of the output file. To make the workflow more user friendly and have more guidance, you will take his model and write a task that will call it. The task will need to allow the user to select some building footprints, then specify a name for the output file. The rest will be done through either the task or the model and be hidden from the user.

1 **Open the project Exercise 7 in the provided materials.**

The project contains several datasets, but the building footprint layer will be the one of interest here. The project also contains a model that the city planner wrote. Start by taking a look at the model to see what it will be doing when you run it.

2 **In the Catalog pane, expand the Toolboxes folder, then expand the Exercise 7.tbx toolbox.**

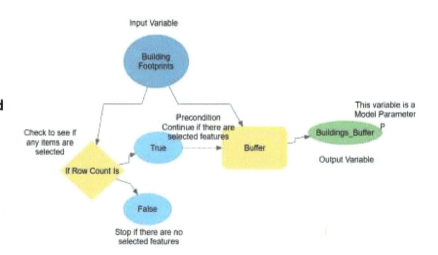

3 **Right click the model 'Buffer selected buildings' and click edit. On the model canvas you will see the components of the model.**

The model that is shown will take the input features (selected building footprints), check to make sure that the selection set isn't zero (using the If Row Count Is function), buffer the items 300' (using the Buffer geoprocessing tool), and create an output feature class that the user was able to name (marked with a P). The dashed line between the Buffer tool and the True output of the logical check is a precondition. It means that the buffer tool will only run when the True output is given. If the logical check is False, the model will stop. If you like, you can double click the logical row count tool or the buffer geoprocessing tool to see how they are set up.

4 **Close the ModelBuilder pane.**

Now that you see how the model works you can build the task that will call it. The task will only need two steps – one that allows the user to select building footprints and one that calls the model.

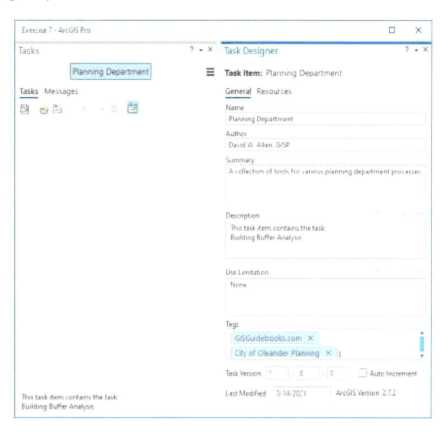

5 Create a new Task Item called Planning Department. Give it a summary as shown in this image.

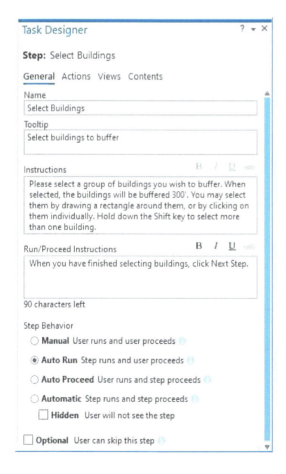

6 Create a new task called Building Buffer Analysis. Add a description based on the scenario description above. Be sure to mention the model that the task will call.

7 Add a new step to the task. Name it Select Buildings and provide other information as shown. Set the step to be Auto Run.

8 Click the Actions tab. Use the record tool to record the Select tool from the Map menu.
Note that the Select command has no parameters to set but you may want to set the Building Footprints to be the only selectable layer.

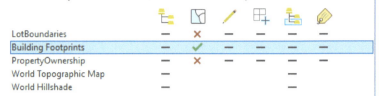

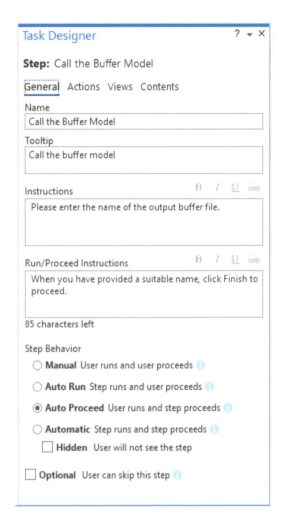

9 Add a new step called Call the Buffer Model with a description as shown. Set the tool to Auto Proceed.

10 Click the Actions tab. On the 'Set the command' line click Edit (pencil icon).

11 Change the Type of Command to Geoprocessing Tool. In the Search pane type in 'Buffer Selected Buildings'. Note that the custom tools from this project are included in the search.

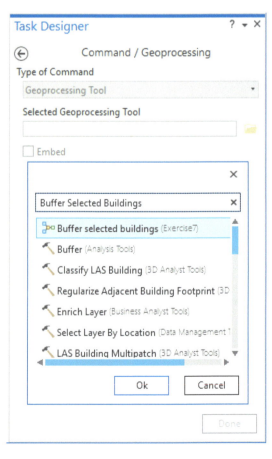

12 Select the Buffer Selected Buildings model and click OK, then click Done.

13 Set this step to only allow selections from the Building Footprints layer by clicking the Contents tab and setting the selection.

14 Close the Tasks Builder pane. Save your project (which will save the tasks).

That's a very simple task, but it is only to demonstrate how to call a model.

15 Expand the Tasks folder and double click Planning Department. Then double click the Building Buffer Analysis task to run it.

16 Move the cursor to the map and draw a selection box around some buildings (it doesn't matter which ones). Then click Next Step.

The task controlled the building footprint selection, and now it is calling the model. Note that the task is showing the step name, step instructions, and run instructions from the task, but is also showing the input parameter from the model.

17 Enter a name for the output file and click Finish. When it completes, close the Tasks pane.

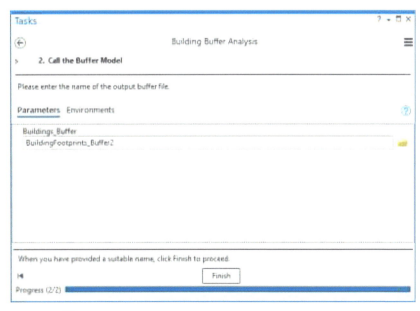

The buffer is created and added to the map. It seems to run just like any other task but remember that you added a tool to make sure the feature count was greater than zero – something that's difficult in a task. Incorporating the model was pretty easy, just make sure that any parameter that you would like the user to define should be made into a parameter within the model (and have a little P next to it).

Rafael's Question—Could you set this up to prompt the user for the buffer distance so that it isn't always 300 feet?

Yes you can! Any parameter from a geoprocessing tool can be made into a model parameter, and thus be shown as input when the task is run. To do this, in the ModelBuilder editing pane you can right click any geoprocessing tool (yellow rectangle) and select Create Variable > From Parameter and a list of the parameters for that tool is shown. Select which parameter you want and it will be made into a blue oval in the model. Then right click that blue oval and select Parameter – it will get a little P. Now your task will prompt for thenew parameter. Try it!

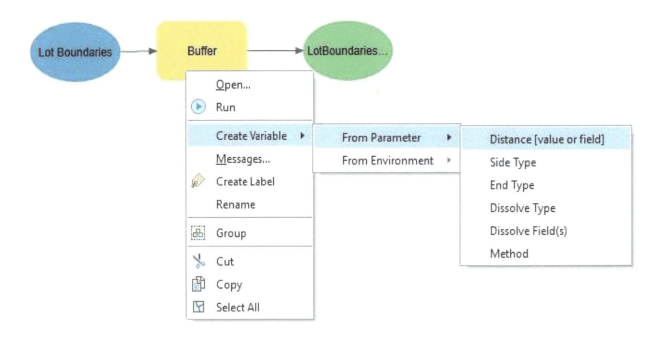

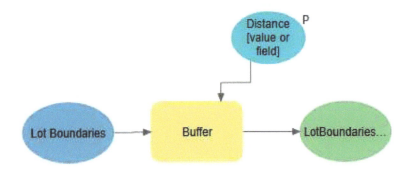

Combining A Model With A Task

The city planner's scenario showed that a task can call a model, and even provide a user defined parameter to the model. The task stopped after the step that included the model, but of course there could be more task steps after the step that included the model. When the model completes, it hands control back to the task which can continue on with more steps.

One thing to watch for, however, is that the model does not encounter any errors. If so, the model will crash and consequently the task will stop. This is why it is important to include error control measures in the model whenever possible – such as the check for the feature count in the last exercise.

Exercise 8 – Waterpark workflow

The last task was rather simple, so it's time to try something more complex. This scenario involves granting the members of a Homeowner's Association (HOA) a discounted rate at the local Splash Town Rodeo, a western themed water park run by the City of Oleander's Parks Department. Citizens of Oleander already get a 20% discount off the standard rate. If an HOA gets more than 20 people to sign up for a summer pass, the city will discount the price by and additional 20% for those households (40% total). And as an additional incentive, areas with an average house value lower than $250,000 will get an additional 10% discount (50% total). Not only that, the park pass also includes free rides on the Dolly Trolley, the Willie Wagon, or the LorettaLink (themed after country music legends Dolly Parton, Willie Nelson, and Loretta Lynn) which run during thesummer months and make stops at 15 locations around town ... including the water park.

The program was started last summer and was wildly successful, and now the Parks Department director wants to automate this workflow – it seems that they have to run the calculations fresh every year because a) the values of the houses may change, b) they have to verify the HOA boundaries, and c) the price of the water park admission may change. In addition, new HOA's are being formed and existing ones expanded just to takc advantage of this offer.

This is what the process will involve:

⇒ A representative will bring in an application for his HOA requesting that their rate be calculated.

⇒ The parks department employee will select a polygon from the HOA feature class.

⇒ All the properties in the HOA will be selected.

⇒ The average house value will be calculated.

⇒ A discounted rate will be calculated based on the average house value and stored in a new field in the HOA feature class.

⇒ As an option, a database of the selected property owners can be exported for the HOA representative. Not all will want this, but for the larger HOA's they may want to send out a flyer in the mail.

⇒ The HOA representative can then take this back to their neighborhood and get residents to sign up.

Take a look at the steps and decide which you feel would best be done with a step in a task vs. calling a model.

First look for things that a model can't do. These things will need to be done by the task. In this scenario, selecting the HOA polygons can't be done in a model. That will have to be a task step. Next look for things a task can't do. Deciding a course of action based on a calculated value can't be done in a task. So deciding which discount to give based on the average property value will have to be done in a model. Then look for any steps that are optional. Models can't do optional steps so that's another job for a task step. The rest of the common functions could be done either way ... YOU decide!

The steps provided below are one way to solve this puzzle and get the application built. Yours may be different, but work it following the book first, then if you want you can build it again using your schematic. The schematic for this solution is:

⇒ Prompt the user to select an HOA polygon

⇒ Step in a task – Select; use the menu tool Select by Rectangle; make sure only HOA polygons can be selected; save the selected feature in a task variable

⇒ Model(1) – Calculate Field; use the calculate field tool and have the user enter the cost of an annual pass; calculate the value into the PassRate field in the HOA polygons layer

⇒ Step in a task – Select by Location; use the Select by location geoprocessing tool; use the selected HOA polygon to select the Property ownership polygons; make sure to use the method "have their center in"; save the selected set in a task variable

⇒ Model(2) – Summary Statistics, use the summary statistics tool to find the average of the field Value2019; save to a temporary table ValTemp

⇒ Model(2) – If Field Value Is; use the If Field Value Is model only tool to determine if the value is greater than or equal to 250000

⇒ Model(2) – Calculate Value; if the previous IF statement is True, calculate the field Discount Rate to 0.4; if the previous IF statement is False, calculate the field Discount Rate to 0.5

⇒ Step in a task - Calculate Field; use the Calculate Field tool to calculate the field PassCost to be PassRate * DiscRate (be sure to recall the selected HOA polygon using the task variable)

⇒ Step in a task - Table to Table; as an option, use the stored task variable to recall the selected property polygons and write them to a user defined table.

You can see that this schematic requires two models. Samples of the models have been supplied, but feel free to write your own versions of the models from scratch. In the steps below, only minimal images are provided to give an overview of the task and models.

The first step was an easy choice – only a task can let the user interact with the map. The second uses a model because the user interface to ask for the cost of the annual pass will look cleaner. If this were done in a task the user would have to build the calculating expression. Then jumping back to the task for the Select by Location lets you use the task variable to store the selected features without creating a new layer. This will come in handy if you need to recall the selection. The second model uses a lot of model only tools to get fieldvalues and do the check to see if it's over $250,000. Then the calculations to the fields in the HOA layer are done in the task because you will need to recall the selected HOA polygon that was saved in the first step. And finally, the optional step to write a table is a step in a task because you will need to recall the saved feature set.

1 **Open the Exercise 8 project.**

You will see the property for Oleander, along with the colored polygons representing the Homeowner Associations. You can see that not all neighborhoods have an HOA, but as word is spreading on the discounted water park pass and free trolley access, there will be more added.

There are two sample models provided. If you aren't comfortable writing your own models, you can use these as-is. But if you have done models before, try using the instructions below and see if you can write yourown (and you can reference the sample models if necessary).

When including a model in a task, it is better to go ahead and create the models first. This will make them visible when you have the task window search for them. At this point they don't need to really do anything,they just need to exist.

2 **Right click the Exercise 8 toolbox in the Catalog pane and select New > Model. When the model is created, right click it and select properties.**

3 **Give it the name "Calculate Fee" along with a tooltip and description.**

4 **Create a second model and call it "Summarize Fields", then provide a tooltip and description.**

With these shell items created you can go ahead and create the task.

5 **Create a new task Item called 'Parks Department Tasks'. You can come back later and dress up the description.**

6 **Within this new task Item, create a new task called 'Calculate Water Park Pass Discount'.**

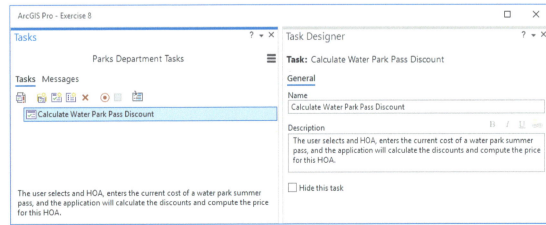

Here are the steps you will need in this task. Note which steps call a model.

⊿   **1. Select the HOA polygon**
     2. Get the standard pass fee ('Calculate Fee' Model)
     3. Select the property
     4. Calculate the Discount Rate ('Summarize Fields' Model)
     5. Calculate pass cost
     6. Export selected property

> *Rafael's Question. Do I have to wait until I'm totally done writing everything before I can test it?*

No – you can try any of these steps or even the models individually before including them in the main task. Many programmers find it easier to debug and fix the small components rather than wait and try to debug the entire process at the end.

Now you can go through this list, creating and configuring each step in the task. When you get to steps 2 and 4 you can go ahead and configure the step to call the models and complete them later.

7 Create a step called 'Select the HOA polygon'

- Set the Step Behavior to AutoRun
- Set the Actions to Select by Rectangle using the Record button
- Add a 'When starting the step' action to Clear Selection
- Add a 'When exiting the step' action to Save Features into SelectedHOA
- Add a 'When exiting the step' verification that only one polygon is selected
- Set Contents so that only the HOA polygons are selectable

8 Create a step called 'Get the standard pass fee'

- Set the Step Behavior to Auto Proceed
- Set the Actions to call the geoprocessing model 'Calculate fee'

9 Create a step called 'Select the property'

- Set the Step Behavior to Automatic (Hidden)
- Set the Actions to 'Select Layer By Location'
- Add a 'When exiting the step' action to Save Features into SelectedProperty

10 Add a step called 'Calculate the Discount Rate'

- Set the Step Behavior to Auto Proceed
- Set the Actions to call the geoprocessing model 'Summarize Fields'

11 Add a step called 'Calculate pass cost'

- Set the Step Behavior to Automatic (Hidden)

- Set the Actions to call the geoprocessing tool Calculate Field

- Set the calculation for the Homeowner Associations table, the Cost of Discounted Pass field, with the calculation: !PassRate! – (!PassRate! * !DiscRate!)

- Add a 'When starting the step' action to Select SelectedHOA

12 Add a step called 'Export selected property'

- Set the Step Behavior to Auto Proceed

- Set the Actions to the geoprocessing tool Table to Table

- Set the InputRows to PropertyOwnership and the Output table to PropertyOwnership_HOA

- Add a 'When starting the step' action to Select SelectedProperty

Phew – there's a few complex steps in there, which just emphasizes how powerful your tasks can be.

With that part done, it's time to write the models. Here's what the first model looks like as a hint. You can either create this on your own or follow the instructions below.

The user enters the fee and it is calculated into a field in the table

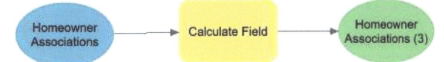

13 Right click the Calculate Fee model and select Edit.

The nice thing about models is that they allow you work with a variable, and as you saw before that variable can be a user defined parameter. To simplify the interface, you will create a variable to accept the standard park pass fee – and that will be the only thing the user sees when the model runs. If this were done through the task the user would have to build the calculation expression, which isn't very user friendly. Note that the name you give the variable will be the prompt in the user interface.

14 Right click anywhere in the model canvas and select Create Variable. Set the data type to Double and click OK.

15 Right click and set it as a model parameter, then right click and rename it to 'Enter Standard Fee'.

16 Finally, double click the variable and set a default value of 200 and click OK.

Next you will need to add the Calculate Field geoprocessing tool to the model. To find the tool, simple click in an open area of the model canvas and begin typing the tool's name. The search box will pop open and you can find the tool. Note – at this writing there is a bug that you can't start a tool search with a capital letter so if you are looking for Calculate Field you should start typing in lower case.

17 Move the mouse to an empty area and type 'calculate field'. Double click the tool in the list to add it to the model.

18 Right click the Calculate Field tool and select Open. Use the drop-down arrow and set the Input Table to Homeowners Association. Set the Field Name to Pass Standard Rate and the calculation to %Enter Standard Fee%. Click OK.

By putting the percent signs before and after the variable name, the tool will substitute the variable value into the calculation.

19 Save and close the model.

Next you will build the summarize Fields model. As you can see in this image the model is fairly complex, but if you break it down into components it won't present such a chore.

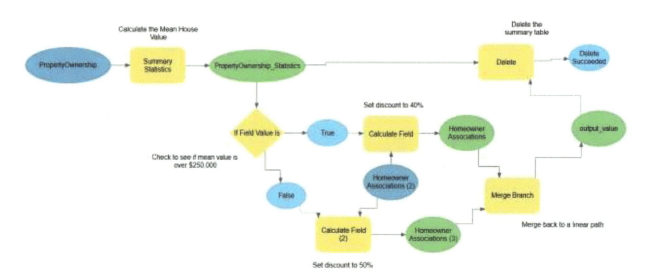

20 Begin editing the Summarize Fields model.

21 Add the Summary Statistics geoprocessing tool. Set the Input table to PropertyOwnership and use the default name for the Output Table. Under the Statistics Field aera, set the Field to Value2019 and the Statistic Type to Mean. Click OK to finish.

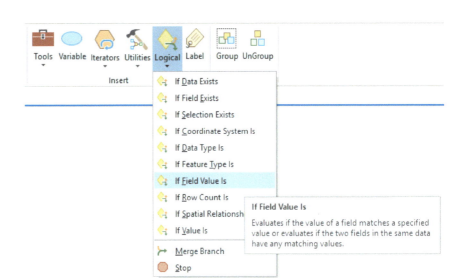

22 **From the Logical tools dropdown menu, find and select If Field Value Is.**

Configuring this logical tool requires three steps. First you set the input table, then you set up a clause that will test the value in a field, and finally you set the selection condition to see if the clause was met. In this case you will work with the PropertyOwner_Statistics summary table. This table will only have one record, and that record will include the field MEAN_Value2019 which represent the average house value from the selected records in the Property Owner layer. If you set a clause to check that the value is more than $250,000, then if it is true there will be one record selected – and conversely if it is less then no records will be selected. So by setting the selection clause to be greater than $250,000 and the selection count to be equal to 1 you will define the True condition. Anything else will be False.

23 **Right click and open the If Field Value Is tool. Use the drop down arrow to set the Input Data Element to PropertyOwnership_Statistics. Then click Clause and the Add Clause button. Build the clauseMEAN_Value2019 is greater than 250000 and click Add.**

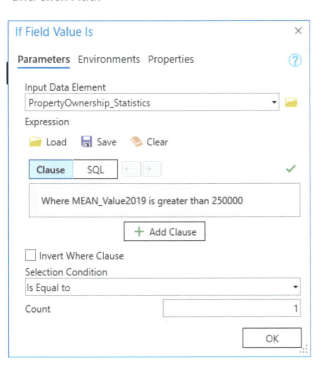

24 **Finally, set the Selection Condition to 'Is Equal to' and the count to 1. Click OK to finish.**

The output will have a True and a False condition. You can set up a calculate field for each condition with True offering a discount of 40% and False offering a discount of 50%. The trick is to use the True and False values as preconditions for the two Calculate Field tools. Don't know how to set a precondition? Check the Help files.

25 **Add a Calculate Field tool to the model. Set the Input Table to Homeowners Association, the Field Name to Discount Rate, and the calculated value to .4. Set the variable True as a precondition for this tool.**

26 **Click OK.**

Add a second Calculate Field tool with the same settings except that the calculated value should be .5 and the precondition should be the False value.

Normally a model takes a straight and linear path, however the If tool created two parallel processes. Only one can run so to get back to a linear path you can use the Merge Branch tool. It's a Model Only tool under the Logical menu and will pass along the value from whichever side of the parallel path is executed. In this case the value doesn't really matter, just the fact that a value was returned is enough.

27 **Add the Merge Branch tool to the model from the Logical menu. It has no parameters to set.**

It would be a good practice to delete the summary table at the end of the model so that when it is run again in the future you won't get an error that the table already exists. This is easy to do but you have to make surethat the table isn't deleted until the set of processes from the If statement have completed. Therefore you can add Delete and make the output of the Merge Branch a precondition of its execution.

28 **Finally, add the Delete geoprocessing tool. Set the output of the Merge Branch tool as a precondition. Save and close the model.**

That's it! Now all the steps in the task are created and configured, and both models are created and configured. It's time to test it.

29 **Move to the Test Area bookmark. Run the task and select the coral colored HOA polygon. Give it a Standard Pass value of $200.**

30 **Now run the task a second time and select the green colored HOA polygon. Use the same Standard Pass value of $200.**

Name	ContactInfo	Pass Standard Rate ▲	Discount Rate	Cost of Discounted Pass
Fuller Station	Warren Fuller	$200.00	0.5	100
Dominion	Shelia Remmington	$200.00	0.4	120

Your task should work perfectly, but in case it didn't you should check the Step Behavior settings. Make sure nothing is hidden that shouldn't be and that all the original setting have been saved. If it still isn't working, you can set up a dummy task and build each step or each model individually and make sure it is working before adding it to the main task.

Rafael's Challenge

This is the last part of the book, and if you've made it this far and gotten all of the exercises completed successfully, then Congratulations!! You should be able to write some pretty great tasks and include models where appropriate. But now the BIG CHALLENGE!!

It seems that Rafael has been doing very well in his GIS class and now he challenges YOU to complete the final two scenarios on your own. You have already learned the techniques and tools necessary to complete them, and each has a scenario description and a rough outline of the process (with hints as to what steps or models you might want to use).

Can you beat Rafael at his own game?

Challenge Number 1

The City of Oleander has seen the appearance of a lawn fungus in some of the residential neighborhoods. The fungus needs to be treated as occurrences are found to prevent it from spreading to other areas. When a homeowner identifies that they may have the fungus, a test is performedand if the lab results are positive then the treatment process begins. You will write a task to automate this process.

First the property is identified by the inspectors and if the property is contaminated, they will give you the GeoReference ID number. Then all residential properties within 100 feet are identified for treatment. However, if a selected property is within the prescribed distance of the source property but is across an expanse of pavement (like a paved road or alley) then it does not have to be
treated since the fungus doesn't bridge the roads very easily. Once all the properties have been properly identified a list of the property addresses and a map of the properties is produced.

Here's a quick schematic of the process:

⇒ Have the user enter a GeoReference ID

⇒ Use the GeoReference ID with Select Layer by Location to select the target property

⇒ Perform a selection around the target property of 100'

⇒ As the user to visually verify the results and unselect any properties that may be across the street (or alley)

⇒ Export the selected features to a table for use in a mail-merge notification letter

⇒ Zoom to the selected properties and produce a small exhibit map

Open the Challenge 1 project and follow these guidelines to build the task. The name and main actions are provided. You will need to add all the details and behaviors. Remember to watch for any selected sets to save or any variables to store.

Step 1 - Activate Map Pane: record the menu tool Activate

The user starts with the layout but has to activate the map pane in order to do the selections

Step 2 – Select the target parcel: Select Layer by Attribute

The user will use the provided GeoReference ID as input for the tool to find the property

Step 3 – Select with buffer: Select Layer by Location

The selected parcel is used to select more parcels. Be sure to use the optional distance setting

Step 4 – Zoom to the selected parcels: Zoom to Selection

Zoom to all the selected property

Step 5 – Unselect property: Rectangle (Interactive Selection)

The user has the opportunity to view and unselect any parcels that are across an expanse of concrete

Step 6 – Export Data: Table to Table

The data for the selected properties is exported to a table.

Step 7 – Pan the layout: Pan to Selection

The map is panned to the selected properties for display on the final map

Step 8 – Close map activation: Close Activation

The control is passed back to the Layout

Step 9 – Add address to title: Properties (Properties of layout text)

The user can type in the property address in the map title

Step 10 – Export layout to PDF file: Export to File …

The completed map is exported to a PDF file for distribution

Now you can test the task. Some sample GeoReference codes that you can use for testing are:

Address	GeoReference ID
306 Newport Cir	46450-4-38
803 Rock Creek Dr	47485-D-21
1505 Cedar Ridge Terr	36700-1-4
213 Edinburgh Dr	11043-B-10

Challenge 2

The Code Services Department has implemented a new inspection process for apartment complexes in Oleander. Each inspector will travel to an apartment complex and run down the checklist of the Minimum Housing Standards. They'd like to have a map of the complexes showing each apartment location, the building footprints, and the actual rental units. All of this data exists, but there is some information that they need that is not in the dataset. For each apartment complex, they need to know how many buildings and how many rental units it contains. Then they need to know the number of rental units each building contains. Finally, they need to have an attribute in the apartment location feature class, the building feature class, and the rental units feature class that contains the CodeID they will assign to each complex.

The process will start when an apartment manager applies for the housing permit and an inspection is scheduled. Code Services will assign a CodeID, and then they will want to find the apartment on a map and calculate the building and unit counts. They've asked for a printed map that they can use to count buildings and units, but it seems that an automated process can be constructed to make this very easy – plus the data can be stored with the features.

Here's a quick schematic of the process:

⇒ Ask the user to select the apartment complex on the map

⇒ Ask the user for the Code ID

◊ Store the CodeID value as a variable for future use

◊ Store the value into the CodeID field of the Apartment Locations layer

⇒ Run the Geoprocessing Tool Select Layer by Location to find the buildings on the property

◊ Store the Code ID value into the CodeID field in the Building Footprints layer

⇒ Have a model:

◊ Count the number of selected buildings (Get Count)

◊ Write the total building count into the NumBldgs field of the

Apartment Locations layer (Calculate Field)

⇒ Run the Geoprocessing tool Select Layer by Location to find the rental units that fall within the selected buildings.

◊ Store the Code ID value into the CodeID field in the Apartment Units layer

⇒ Have a model:

- ◊ Count the number of selected rental units (Get Count)
- ◊ Write the rental unit count into the NumUnits field of the Apartment Locations layer (Calculate Field)

⇒ Have a model:

- ◊ Iterate through the selected set of buildings (Iterate Features)
- ◊ Select the rental units in each building (Select Layer by Location)
- ◊ Count the number of units within each building (Get Count)
- ◊ Write the rental unit count into the NumUnits field of the Building Footprints Layer (Calculate Field)

You will develop a Task for this using task features and models, and as each permit application is received the inspectors will work up one apartment complex. Eventually they will visit each complex and run the task for each. This process may take three inspectors many years to complete, sohaving the task will ensure that the process is done the same way over the years.

Open the Challenge 2 project and follow these guidelines to build the task and models. The name and main actions are provided along with an image of the completed models. You will need to add all the details and behaviors. Remember to watch for any selected sets to save or any variables to store.

⇒ Step 1 – Select apartment complex: Rectangle (Interactive Selection)

- ◊ The user selects the apartment complex by clicking on it with the mouse

⇒ Step 2 – Get CodeID: Get Attributes / Additional Action: Calculate CodeID into table

- ◊ A value is retrieved from the attribute table and calculated into the ApartmentLocations layer

⇒ Step 3 – Select the buildings: Select Layer by Location / Additional Action: Calculate CodeID into table

- ◊ Use the selected ApartmentLocations polygon to select included buildings and calculate the CodeID into the BuildingFootprints layer

⇒ Step 4 – Building Count (Model): Get Count / Select Layer by Location / Calculate Field

◊ The model counts the number of buildings, then calculates the value into the ApartmentLocations polygon

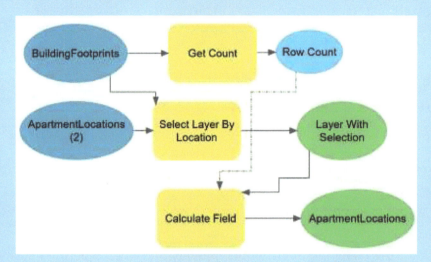

⇒ Step 5 – Select the rental units: Select Layer by Location / Additional Action: Calculate CodeID into apartment units layer

◊ The apartment units within the selected polygon are themselves selected and the CodeID value is transferred to the table

⇒ Step 6 – Count the Rental Units (Model): Get Count / Select Layer by Location / Calculate Field

◊ The model counts the number of rental units, then calculates the value into the ApartmentLocations polygon

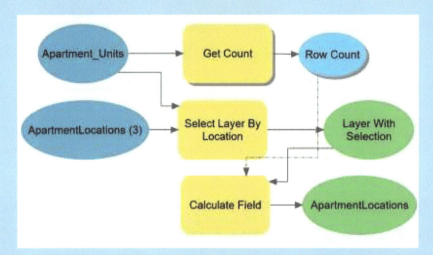

⇒ Step 7 – Select the buildings: Select Layer by Location

◊ The buildings are selected again because the previous selection will have been cleared

⇒ Step 8 – Count Units per Building (Model): Iterate Feature Selection / Get Count / Select Layer by Location / Calculate Field

◊ The model counts the number of rental units per building, then calculates the value into the BuildingFootprints layer

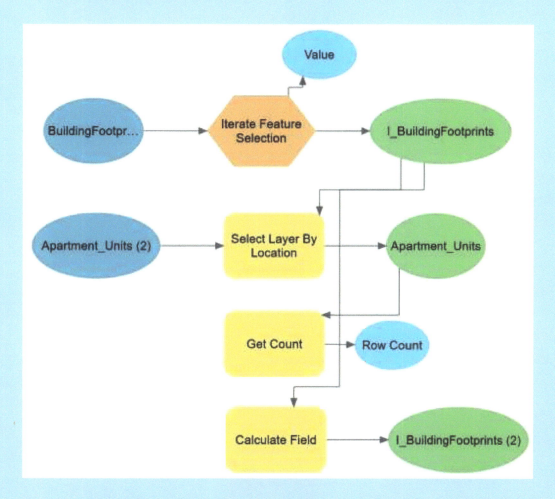

WooHoo! That completes the model. Take THAT, Rafael.

Test the task by zooming and selecting any apartment complex, then supply any sort of ID code, such as APT24A or APT45Y.

That wraps it up. You are NOW a Task Master!! DWA